D1831648

PRIMITIVE TRIBAL GROUPS IN EASTERN INDIA
Welfare and Evaluation

PRIMITIVE TRIBAL GRUOUPS IN EASTERN INDIA
Welfare and Evaluation

P.K. BHOWMICK

GYAN

Primitive Tribal Groups in Eastern India
(Anthropology, Tribal Studies)

© P.K. Bhowmick

ISBN: 81-212-0465-8
Library of Congress Card No.93-90029

All rights reserved. No part of this book may be reproduced in any manner without written permission.

Reprinted in 2013 in India by
Gyan Publishing House
23, Main Ansari Road, Daryaganj,
New Delhi - 110002
Phone : 23282060, 23261060
Fax : (011) 23285914
E-mail : books@gyanbooks.com
Website: gyanbooks.com

Printed at: G. Print Process, Delhi

PREFACE

To quote an excerpt from the report of a bureaucrat--

> For quite sometime past, it was a major issue of discussion in the District Welfare Committee for Scheduled Castes and Scheduled Tribes that haphazard investment of money at Totopara has proved to be quite futile and such unplanned schemes have so far failed to bring the desired changes in the production system and living standard of the Totos.
>
> Balagopal, Commissioner: (1982).

This might be the reaction of other senior officers also at different places of West Bengal where the tribals, specially the backward section of them live, and all these pieced together might be cogent cause for agony for many thinkers and Scientists, including the Social Scientists working in the field. The Government of India spent tons of money in the hope and belief of doing the welfare work among these people. Below is a synopsis of the recent Central Government grants released for such welfare activities in West Bengal which will give a casual observer a cursory picture of the tribal development situation in this part of our country.

The position of released amount for PTG in West Bengal State during 6th and 7th plan period.

Year	Amount (Rupees in lakhs)	
1980-81	5.00	
1981-82	10.00	
1982-83	11.00	
1983-84	24.85	Total amount
1984-85	24.85	during 7th
1985-86	25.00	plan period
1986-87	27.68	Rs. 152.99
1987-88	27.74	lakhs.
1988-89	30.57	
1989-90	42.00	

Source: Tribal Development - a statistical profile, Tribal Development Division, Ministry of Welfare.

There are altogether 476 tribal communities with a total population of 5,16,26,638 according to 1981 census. Out of this, the Primitive Tribal Groups in West Bengal number 3 technically, but they are actually considered 4 (four), namely-1. Toto (852), 2. Birhor (165), 3. Lodha (approx. 26,000), 4. Kheria/Kharia (approx. 8,000).

Next Table indicates total grant released for all the Scheduled Tribe population of West Bengal from the Central Government.

GRANTS RELEASED
(Special Central Assistance)

	1989-90 (Rupees in lakhs)
I.T.D.P	681.00
Outside I.T.D.P.	205.00
M.A.D.A.	-
Cluster	-
Primitive Tribes	42.00
Margin Money	55.70
Special Schemes	-
Additional for minor irrigation of primitive tribes schemes.	32.88
Total	1,016.58

After independence, provisions were made to upgrade the living standard of these people in various ways, for which both Central and State Governments, sanctioned grants. Casual Voluntary Organisations, Governmental outfits and lastly the democratically elected Panchayats took over the welfare/development activities, not only to ameliorate the economic conditions but also to make them conscious about their role in the democratic set up, through imparting education and other socialisation processes.

The above mentioned groups have distinctive ways of life, socio-cultural background to be able to absorb various shocks in course of historical interactions. Naturally, therefore, the welfare activities, in order to bring about stable changes may be varied and different in nature. Various Commissions and their recommendations after comparative studies of the conditions of all these tribes have portrayed a rather bleak picture of some of the tribal groups, who number 74 (in 1990) in India to be considered as the Primitive Tribal Groups (PTG) of which West Bengal claims only 3, viz., Toto, Birhor, Lodha/Kheria being considered one group though the Lodhas and the Kherias/ Kharias are two culturally distinct groups of people. The main criterion to designate a PTG are - their numerically small number, their living in comparatively geographical isolation, their growth rate appearing abnormally low compared to other tribal population, pre-agricultural level of technology and extremely low level of literacy. (Report of the Working Group : 1984). Of course, the Dhebar Commission (1961) referred to these groups as the 'lowest layer' among the Scheduled Tribe communities.

All these groups, now being considered as Primitive Tribal Groups, are getting financial assistance, educational priorities, facilities of drinking water and housing, other routine programmes on special considerations, from time to time. Special grant from the Government of India was naturally allotted for them since 1980-81 as they were treated as PTG by which, within a stipulated period, they can overcome the prevailing constraints. The administration also sincerely wanted to look into the situation, as to how far all these grant and possibilities could match between each other to elevate their condition and, as such, a systematic study is needed. These developments must have certain goals or targets touching everybody of the groups. Therefore, an evaluation on the part of the administration becomes imperative. It cannot, however, be denied that evaluation of a long-drawn welfare programme meant for these groups, having distinctive socio-cultural background, out of Government grants indicates the necessity for assessment of the development done so far in reality for achieving the goal by gradually changing the cultural particularly in the matter of building up of organisations, accommodation, making cautious tests about the social groups in and around them and toning up the ethos.

Accordingly, the Ministry of Welfare (T.D. Department), Govt. of India was approached and Sri B.K. Mishra, IAS, the then Joint Secretary, took up the case and as a consequence sanctioned a sum of Rs. 52,000/- [vide No.15025/23/88-TD (R)] for embarking upon such a project in West Bengal. Three Fellow/Scholars were engaged on the job for a period of ten months to see through the project under operation. Smt. Krishna Mazumdar, Smt. Chandrima Chanda and Shri Gautam Mallick, were recruited for the purpose and DR. (Mrs.) Samita Manna as Co-Director; Shri P. Chowdhury, IAS, Secretary, SC and ST Department, Govt. of West Bengal; Dr. A.K. Das, Director, Research Institute; Shri G. Balachandhrana, IAS, District Magistrate and Collector, Midnapur; Shri M.N. Roy, IAS, District Magistrate and Collector, Jalpaiguri; Shri K. Bhowmick, S.D.O., Jalpaiguri; Shri D. Gautam, S.D.O., Jhargram; Shri I. Iswarari, Project Officer, I.T.D.P, Jalpaiguri. Shri S. Mondal and Shri D. Das, Project Officers, I.T.D.P., Jhargram; Shri N. Bhattacharya, Project Officer, I.T.D.P., Purulia; Shri A. Rashid, Project Officer, Bankura and many other B.D.O.'s and concerned government officials, in conjunction with us, for whose services, I owe a word of thanks to them all. They ungrudgingly complied with the requests to let us handle all the audited accounts, of expenditures, since 1980-81. After getting these, our Research Fellows went to the respective Block offices to have the villages and see the beneficiaries. Sometimes our scholars had to face difficulties while meeting the beneficiaries in remote villages. Superintendent of Chaksahapur Ashram Hostel Midnapur, initially gave statement and allowed us but while in the next time refused to speak without the permission of the panchayat regarding the Ashram Hostels meant for the Lodha boys and girls.

However, the basis of this team of workers was to verify the nature of problems and the welfare strategies meant for the tribal people concerned, and how far the groups are in a position to take in their problems realistically. Moreover, how far the welfare agencies and the interaction of the groups in question are in a position to assimilate the developmental benefits for them and how such a spirit of self-reliance has been generated among them. Problems have been discussed with the team; the agencies of welfare and their *modus operandi* have been dwelt on at length critically and, last but not the least, some corrective steps have been suggested, so as to circumvent the difficulties surfaced in course of implementation of the welfare measures with a view to strengthen the adaptive base in terms of ecology and environment, vis-a-vis age group distribution and family sizes, and in this way the absorbing capacity is extended beyond the traditional ecology-cum-economic and historio-politico situations bringing these groups at least in the scope of functional literacy and widening their world view.

However, for this purpose small tribes, like the Toto (family 163), have been studied in-depth and verified along with the families of other tribal groups. Similar action has been taken in respect of the Birhors (family 47) who are small in number in West Bengal. But, with regard to the Kheria/Kharia (family 216) and the Lodha (family 288) sample families have been studied through a particular project. How far these welfare activities and their concommitant benefits have seeped through the tribal groups concerned and elevated their existing socio-economic stratum has to be measured.

Though from the Government side we got all the help and co-operation possible, sometimes joint ventures to verify the situation had made in collaboration with the Government officials and the researching team. But, unfortunately, some amount of non co-operation is at times noticeable from the side of Panchayats in charge of such welfare programme. The attitude of the Zilla Parishad Chairman, i.e., the Sabhadhipati who is considered the top democratic boss to look after the welfare activities in the districts is not very happy, inasmuch as he considers it out of fashion to reply to our letters and reminders except the Sabhadhipati of the district of Bankura.

In a separate chapter in this report, a suggestion has been made that constant field studies, verification of facts and co-ordination of all the findings should be made for better implementation and execution of the projects.

In this connection, I would like to put on record my gratefulness to Sarbashree G.S. Nair, former Under Secretary, P.K. Mohanty, Dy. Director Research Wing (TD), D.K. Ray, Dy. Director (TD), R.C. Mohapatra, Research Officer, Ministry of Welfare, all of Govt. of India, New Delhi. My academic friends Sarbashree Bimalendu Majumdar of Jalpaiguri and Gokul Chandra Deb of Midnapur, who took keen interest in helping me bring out this book in various ways, also deserve my thankfulness. Dr. M.K. Raha, Joint Director, Anthropological Survey of India, Calcutta took interest to publish this volume and it has been materialised due to sincere effort of Sri B.P. Garg, the Chief Executive and Sri S.N. Sarkar, Editor of the Gyan Publishing House, I sincerely thank them all.

Bidisa
Delhi.

P.K. BHOWMICK

CONTENTS

Part One

BACKGROUND

1

Introduction

India is inhabited by varied groups of people, having not only of different physical features but also of divergent life styles. This is mainly true to her typical geographical setting which has left a profound impact on their life and living and also the action pattern. Lack of communication facilities in certain periods of time among these groups in some areas which are yet to be overcome through positive communication processes, even after this forty years of Indian Independence of our welfare state through spread of education and by democratic means or participation in the nation building activities. India is a welfare state and this is the be-all and end-all of all our activities. The founding fathers of the Indian Constitution, most of whom were engaged in the struggle for freedom against the foreign rule, had their acquaintance with the so-called stratified people, high and low or rich and poor, allowed themselves to be considered more critically and sympathetically. They understood the problems arising out of their illiteracy, more tradition bound mentality, non-responsiveness to modern thinking and such other things which are associated with the factors that prompted them and their representatives to feel the pangs of the conditions of being underprivileged groups. Thus, the elites and thinkers of our country made provisions in the Indian Constitution not only to extend various welfare or developmental activities for the upliftment of the down-trodden through financial support of the Government. It has been laid down in Article 339 of the Constitution in this connection that:

> The President may in any time and shall at the expiration of ten years from the commencement of the Constitution by order appoint a Commission to report etc. etc.

Pursuant to this, there were successive commissions, sometimes to examine special issues, sometimes to evaluate the nature of developmental activities which are expected to be reflected in these reports. They tried to examine the local needs and locate the geniuses from amongst the people, specially the so-called tribal groups for whom the development is meant, through the Constitutional provisions. In most of the cases, when the problems surfaced, the culture of the target groups is more meaningfully studied and the operating administrative mechanism are clearly brought to bear upon it to know the people's reactions. The immediate results are scrutinised for understanding these developmental procedures systematically. As a result, monitoring or mid-term evaluation is a must, for, this can interpret many more well known situations, specially interacting with the traditions of the people's attitudes towards development programmes and also the agencies of development or implementation of the schemes, either through Government officials or by the Panchayat personnel representing democracy or NGO's (Non-Government Organisations) involved for the overall betterment of these people. We can easily understand that for such groups of people plans and policies are formulated with the desire of implementation, in most cases, with Government funds. It is also implied that meaningful discussions about the socio-economic conditions and the traditions of the people should constitute one of the vital materials. The core part of development as a socio-economic growth presupposes a condition in which human resources are transformed into a source of creative activity and we believed that it is the foundation of all development strategies. Sometimes, the cost of various development strategies raises a question in the mind of the administrators at the top level, along with the social scientists involved in studying the groups and also the interested persons here and there - many more apprehensions and local criticisms are constellated to prove the situation clearly, with the simple question of what is happening and how far the new deal is needed for promoting a change for the better through all these developmental activities done for the groups. Of course, this will automatically correlate changes in the social structure, political set-ups as well as cultural values of the target groups along with the persons involved in the welfare activities. This will undoubtedly strengthen the process of understanding the situation by promoting the initiatives and awareness of the grassroot level by broadening and accommodating the emerging groups of people on the one hand and imparting education on the other, involving participation by toning up the processes of scientific study of the cultural life, that includes their moral, ethical and developing machinery of the personnel composition and, above all, the contents of plan strategies and their nature of realistic approaches to people for whom all the money is being spent, and the man-power is engaged. Thus, through evaluation processes, we shall be in a better position to know primarily the people, their culture, their immediate needs and perception of a better life style along with the nature of response and reaction. Keeping all these in mind if we proceed, then we shall be able to find out the causes of successes and failures of developments, whether these would create more employment opportunities on the one hand and the higher echelons of development administration on the other and realise the existing communication gap between the people and the efficient functionaries along with the operating democratic flag-bearers involved with the welfare activities for the betterment of the groups concerned at the cost of the Central Government money.

II

The Indian Constitution describes some groups of people as a 'Weaker Section', because in various ways those groups (either caste or tribe) are not in a position to compete with their stronger brethren. Some of them are euphemistically called 'tribes'. Of them, the 'Bhumi-Putras' (sons of the soil or autochthonese) are known as 'Adivasis' or the 'early settlers' to the general mass. They are, as per the Constitution, called the Scheduled Tribes. The total number of these communities is 476 and the total population figure, according to 1991 Census, is 6,77,58,380. Most of them have distinctive life - styles of their own, which are sometimes symbolised through their language and culture. It is said that some of them were pushed back to the remotest parts of the unhealthy terrain of our country, just to eke out their existence when they were faced with an alien government or scheming people, having better technology. Article 342 of our Constitution enjoins that the tribes are entitled to have development benefits, provided they are 'Scheduled'. The President, by his special power, specifies some groups as 'Scheduled Tribes' or

> "the tribes or the tribal communities or the parts of or groups within the tribes and Tribal Communities by a public notification".

All these Scheduled Tribal groups are entitled to have many benefits directly from the Government, along with many other opportunities in respect of economic development, educational facilities, improvement of basic requirement in connection with health, communication etc. They are not to be exploited and some of their tribal traditions are to be respected, specially in the areas where the Sixth Schedule is operative. There is a provision for reservation for them, not only in Government service but also in Assembly and Parliamentary seats. Many of them live below the poverty, having no job facilities or any source of income due to lack of proper education and training. It is desired that they should be pulled out of their present quagmire without any disturbance to their traditional life - style or basic philosophy, i.e., which kept them from unseemly greed from material possessions. It is of course a fact that these groups of people have been cheated outright by many, specially during the British rule, so much so that their discontent had burst out in the form of armed revolt and insurrections in many places, in the past. There have been various instances much revolts from all over the country and, naturally, the then British Government in power maintained a policy of *laissez faire* about them. However, it has been unmistakably proved that these people live at widely different stages of development, because some of them have specific economy, primitive technology and less acquaintance with the wider spectrum of the society in and around them. Generally, through many plans and programmes of various welfare measures the Government tried to tackle their problems with a view to raising their standard of living, i.e., from poverty to prosperity, from ill-health or malnutrition to sound and vigorous sparkling life, making provision of food, drinking water and also making them fit for receiving the modern methods of medical treatment. Through imparting education by providing schools, hostel accommodation, granting stipends and many other beneficial programmes, and raising their standard of living, they can be made suitable for taking up white-collar jobs, like any other groups of people, and they can be helped to come out with flying colours from their narrow environments. The educational facilities will bring among them a new awakening supplanting their present inferiority complex and will weave a sense of integrity with all these bright ideas, the Government of India not only sanctioned benevolent grants but also brought in their representatives in the natioin-building work extending to many more welfare schemes with a realistic approach. So, we find provision of Government grants sanctioned for development strategies vary from time to time in different plan periods, only to achieve healthy transformation, enabling them to enjoy all the facilities extended to all other groups of people. Thus, development or welfare became a fundamental, strategy for these people who are apparently lagging behind the other advanced communities of our country. After independence, their problems were studied in various ways and the remedial measures were suggested to bring in a fruitful change, but to many it is not upto their expectations. Naturally, development is considered a dynamic and model phenomenon as it implies change from one level to another - suggested indirectly a stage of transformation from traditionalism to modernism. The role of cultural contact and the resultant social changes is also considered a process of development.

III

Records show that the first tribal sub-plan was conceived in 1974-75 in which incisive approach to the problems of the tribal people was throughout necessary. Before that, different Universities, Research Organisations and the Minisrty of Welfare (formerly the Ministry of Home Affairs, TD) took initiative not only in problem-oriented researches but also in many action plans. Besides, various Institutes, both Government. and non-Government., became interested in studying the problems organising seminars and workshops. Thus the problems of the tribals were more surfaced clearly and were visible. A good number of ethnographic books, seminar proceedings of varied nature were made available due to the encouragement given by the Government. indicating that these problems should not be allowed to *deift* endlessly. We also find escalation in the total plan outlay during these Plan Periods. **(Report of the Working Group on Development of Scheduled Tribes During the 7th Five Year Plan : P.2).** Of course, provisions were made for implementation and monitoring of the tribal sub-plan programme. Family oriented schemes for removal of poverty, specially among the Scheduled Tribes, became a thrust issue during the Sixth Plan. In this connection, it has been stated : (*ibid* : p.4) :

> Monitoring and evaluation of programmes had not received adequate attention during the Fifth Plan on account of which a lot of difficulty was experienced later to measure its achievement in an intelligible and meaningful manner. This lapse was sought to be rectified by systematising the procedure for monitoring during the Sixth Plan period by seeking to spread the net of evaluation over a good number of projects and schemes.

However, we shall have to take it into consideration that in many cases the problems of each group of people, as also the nature of their perception, varies. Some people live more or less in isolated terrain, whereas others live in more interesting scenes. When a good number of these so-called Scheduled Tribes are concentrated at one place, having more than 50% of their population, the areas are known as Scheduled areas (only in the Fifth Schedule). In the Scheduled areas, the tribals are dominated and as such they are expected to enjoy their existing rights over land. Implementation of tribal development plan through changing economy and technology, educational and social progress of the people are given priorities. Along with these psycho-emotional aspects of their culture is not overlooked for considering their overall development. Now, from the long list of tribes, only 74 communities have been categorised as 'Primitive Tribal Groups' (PTG) due to various factors, namely, those who live in more isolation, having pre-agricultural level of technology and extremely low standard of literacy. Most of these communities are numerically very small, some are at the brink of total annihilation. Dhebar Commission (1961) referred to them as the *lowest layer* of the Scheduled Tribe communities. During the Fifth Five Year Plan period, Ministry of Home Affairs identified 52 such groups as Primitive Tribal Groups having an estimated population of approximately 10 lakhs, while in the Sixth Plan period 20 other communities were added and, again, two came in; thus, the number of such groups came to 74, state-wise in all. The Kharias of West Bengal have been dropped out from the list **(Report of the Working Group on Development and Welfare of the Scheduled Tribes During Eighth Five Year Plan 1989: p. 105)** though in Bihar and Orissa they are included. We have to accept that most of these Primitive Tribal Groups have very specific styles of living. Due to encapsulated and dominating ecology, their life style differs, consequent upon less communication facilities have also put them in an unenviable position, and all these taken together have cut for them a deep gorge into their life style. Accordingly, the people have to roll down helplessly into it. However, various welfare measures to pitchfork them in a system of affluence were made, viz., health, hygiene, education and also to save them from the exploitation of the money-lending sharks. Implementation of these schemes, being done not only by the Government agencies but also by some voluntary organisations, who were involved in the work, to raise their standard of living and to develop a better hygienic condition and to impart education through *Ashram* type schools which automatically allowed them to live in a better way of mixing with the so-called neighbouring groups. Thus, on the one hand they will try to understand the meaning of the welfare measures through plans and projects along with alternative vocational views and on the other they can realise the well-meaning endeavours of the Government. These planned welfare activities and other developmental work undoubtedly allow them to be accommodated with the other bigger societies around them. It is important to note here that all financial grants are being made available to the groups by the Central Government. These people, before they were categorised as Primitive Tribal Groups, had the advantage of getting the benefits meant for all the tribals, but nothing extra. But special provision was made when they were categorised as 'PTG' and the entire amount was sanctioned by the Central Government. It is reported (1984 : 91) that:-

> The Ministry of Home Affairs has reported that a review conducted by them after programmes suggest that the States have not geared as yet their machinery approximately to take up relevant programmes adequately for the groups. They have also indicated that preparation of detailed project has lagged behind,... though the Ministry continues to finance these programmes on full grant basis.

Considering the nature of problems and their unending constraints of varied nature, the Central Government also became extremely alert, cautious and realised that (*ibid* : 90) :

> Public and voluntary agencies should share the responsibility of the care of nursing of the primitive tribal groups along with the governmental agencies. Partnership of the voluntary sector can impart to it a sensitivity and responsiveness which lacks otherwise. We would therefore appeal to the non-governmental organisations to come forward on their own to accept the challenge.

Nevertheless, the group recommended many items (*vide* pages 92-94) as guidelines which were meant for the welfare of the Primitive Tribes in general, as the entire grant was being released by theCentral Government.

IV

The basic import of the word 'development' is a process which means movement from a condition towards another, process of gradual unfolding or 'growth' 'or stage of advancement'. It sums up and designates the most important aspects of changes concerning the 'well-being' or 'uplift' of the people, in general, and it ensures stability-cum-comfort in the living processes. Undoubtedly, development is an active policy which refers to 'mature economy' and 'self-sustaining growth', and the related action pattern will no doubt generate an increased productivity which, in course of time, will improve the quality of life, namely, elevating the people from poverty to prosperity and opening up more employment opportunities, setting apart more leisure time by which their creative art and philosophy can be reflected in finer things, diseases can be checked and ignorance can be removed, if the group is allowed to have a privileged life style. It is true that many more welfare activities have been extended to all the tribal groups, i.e., plans have been drawn up with the help of experts or, perhaps, in consultation with the leaders of democratic political parties, who have vested interest and local support of their followers for whom such benefits are meant. The politicians of all times and climates try to gain control over the power and resources. If we illegally succumb to their pressures, then we deviate from the path of actual development. It is expected that in order to achieve success in development we shall have to consider :

(i) The plans and the agencies formulating it as to whether they have an unbiased and clear idea about the culture of the people as well as their ecological setting, their history and tradition;

(ii) Understanding of the people with their culture entity, their image profile, mental make-up, along with their response to the developing or external situation. These should be well understood while formulating the plan;

(iii) The implementing agency must be able to tackle the people during the development work, as also the Government bureaucrats;

(iv) To keep provision for changing the plan or welfare programme, if found unsuitable or if it retards the growth;

(v) To keep provision for regular monitoring with the help of experts in time and seeking from them constructive suggestions if needed.

Naturally, the success of any development projects or welfare activities depend on all the above factors, in which a clear co-ordination of all the sectors, viz., the governmental machinery, implementing agency, people's participation is the first pre-requisite. In this State, we have a permanent department of Commissioners of Scheduled Castes and Scheduled Tribes, which is also in existence in other States. There are Cultural Research Institutes with expert hands to look after the situation. They are supposed to examine and to report, if and when necessary. Still the Ministry of Welfare has provided for evaluation of many projects meant for the welfare of the tribal people. The people, or the beneficiaries or the target group, are of prime importance. We have to accept that many more programmes or projects have been drawn up for them, specially in case of the Primitive Tribal Groups, because their entire financial grant is being received from the Central Government.

Evaluation of development programmes is an imperative necessity not only to guide the persons involved in but also to indicate the approximation of the success made, and in such a situation evaluation of any welfare programme is a must. It has been mentioned previously that the development programme should be made keeping in view the psycho-emotional and the cultural backdrop of the people, and also by considering the physio-ecological background of the area *vis-a-vis* the structure of the neighbouring communities. It is to be examined how far exploitation by the *guilible* and scheming money-lenders is continuing even today in various parts of the country and this cancerous growth among the simple tribal people must be countered forthwith. Further, we shall have to accept that success of development programmes largely depends on the five factors mentioned above along with the nature of bureaucratic set up as against the crawling democratic ignorance which often hinders the growth of the programmes, namely the corruption and jobbery of such people who want things to be done according to their sweet-will. We shall have to take care always of these practical difficulties and this will be understandable only through unprejudiced evaluation of such programmes. As it has been seen that penury generates power, helping the poor is therefore necessary who toe the poverty line.

In this connection, it can be said that the evaluation of programmes meant for a group requires a clear understanding or conceptualisation of the design, of the implementing agency, of the responsive nature of the targetted groups and their cultural constraints. Complete surrender of the people to a situation which is controlled by the leaders of some democratic political parties must be kept in check. Naturally, it refers to a facets of the problem, the population structure with its historiocity, eco-phyisical background and the forces of other ethnic groups around them. We shall have to understand the conceptualisation and the design analysis, cost-benefit ratio, intervention by the scheming or designing persons, changing of programmes in case of failures and regular monitoring with suggestions of remedial measures. Undoubtedly, the person who knows the anatomy of the society properly, who knows the people from a close range and who has a scientific outlook will be in a better position to evaluate than others and to identify areas where the rot begins. While evaluating a programme, we must not ignore the role of the target groups, their socio-cultural background and the capability of their understanding the problem as well as the procedure of the development programme operation. We shall have to take into account the wider economic perspective as also the political climate of the State, the pressure points and their role in implementing the programme in relation to the situations of the target groups. The reflection of their views through economic approaches and other hindering aspects can be visualised through the whole spectrum of development programme, which can be made in a realistic manner. All this will clear the cob-webs in the background, help assess the actual need of the target group and the maximum utilisation of the manpower and proper training of the personnel of the executing organisation which will deliver the good result. Thus, evaluation of any programme will save many wastages in time, money and energy, just to bring in the target groups in tune with the bigger society around them with an idea to integrate and remove the supposed inequality.

V

Social scientists associated with the action oriented researches or evaluating a project or programmes must not forget that co-ordination of the people with the implementing agencies, the administrative heads and their role in the matter, will not only bring about the desired changes but also will harmonise the situation wholly. In this connection, we should not forget that :

> ....theory and practice are related to each other and knowledge and action go together and the objective of research was to produce usable knowledge. We believe, as all of you undoubtedly do, that knowledge and action should be mutually supplementary and complementary.

(Dubashi: 1983 : IV)

It is an undeniable fact that the development programme should always be time-bound and we must not keep the people submerged in the abysmal depth of poverty for all times, which as in the ultimate analysis brought them insecurity in their socio-economic life. This is more so because, Government has been spending a lot of money for their upliftment. As it is now, we must not treat them as vermins-a grant-receiving beggars, so to say, open to be exploited by the wily politico-social leaders. Though we believe in democratic leaders and think that they should have control over the powers and resources for the benefit of the people, in general, and doling out small favours here and there to them, this is not considered healthy in a wider perspective. They should try to generate power for more and more of employment opportunities and thus eradicate the regional and sub-regional disparities. Thus, enthusiastic attempts will come out to modernise or instill a middle class norm in the mind of the people of the target groups with a nationalistic bent of mind. Socio-psychological background, tribal-cultural and traditionalism should be inculcated in them to make them happy and unified. The twin approach of -

(1) respect for cultural values of the tribals, and

(2) raising their level of living through the instrumentality of developmental measures in plans and projects or programmes initiated by the government and implemented by the organisations, as also getting actual response through realisation of self-sufficiency will prove the extent of success.

However, repetitive mistakes should be avoided and corrective measures taken from the past experiences. Sometimes, old welfare formulae of the democratic bosses of the grass-root level and dominated by the people in power mislead or make inactive the responsible trained officers. At times, this kind of silence or withdrawal attitude or detachment from the situation, dampens their spirit and allow the poverty, exploitation and disbelief to get the better of their ignorance and inability. Naturally, evaluation should be treated as a healthy sign of growth, which can offer alternatives and dispell various suspicious and apprehensions. This will also keep at bay the vested interests and clear the cob web of ignorance of the people from the scenario of welfare programmes. The benefits of evaluation will rectify the mistakes and improve the destiny of the down-trodden who are the victims of an age-old tradition enmeshed in poverty and helplessness at the hands of the local pseudo-politicians.

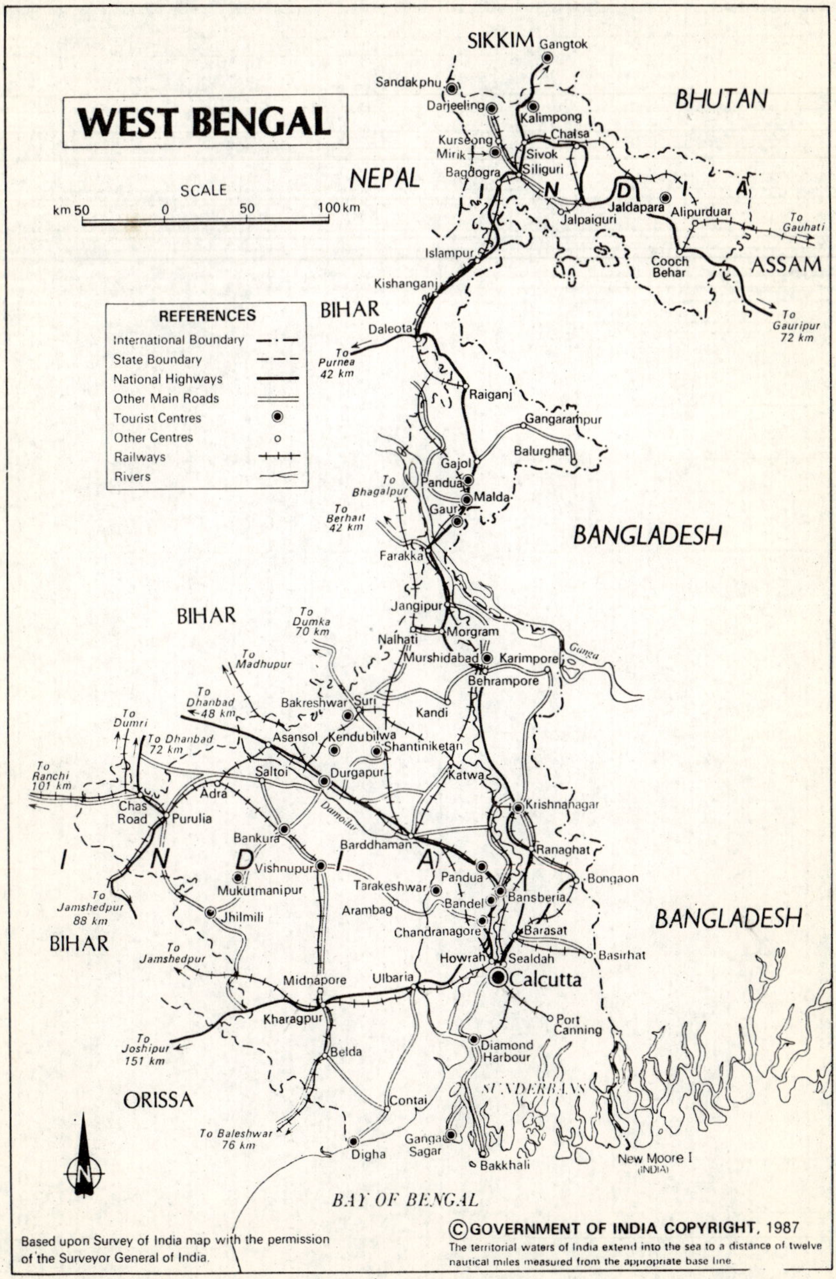
WEST BENGAL
SCALE
km 50 0 50 100 km
REFERENCES
International Boundary
State Boundary
National Highways
Other Main Roads
Tourist Centres
Other Centres
Railways
Rivers
SIKKIM
Gangtok
Sandakphu
Darjeeling
Kalimpong
BHUTAN
Chalsa
Kurseong
Mirik
Sivok
Siliguri
Bagdogra
NEPAL
I N D I A
Jaldapara
Alipurduar
Jalpaiguri
To Gauhati
Islampur
Cooch Behar
ASSAM
Kishanganj
BIHAR
To Gauripur 72 km
Daleota
To Purnea 42 km
Raiganj
Gangarampur
Balurghat
Gajol
To Bhagalpur
Pandua
Malda
To Berhait 42 km
Gaur
BANGLADESH
Farakka
Jangipur
BIHAR
To Dumka 70 km
Nalhati
Morgram
Ganga
To Madhupur
Murshidabad
Karimpore
Behrampore
To Dhanbad 48 km
Bakreshwar
Suri
Kandi
To Dumri
To Dhanbad 72 km
Asansol
Kendubilwa
Shantiniketan
To Ranchi 101 km
Saltoi
Durgapur
Katwa
Adra
Chas Road
Purulia
Damodar
Krishnanagar
Bankura
Barddhaman
Ranaghat
I N D I A
Vishnupur
Pandua
Bongaon
Mukutmanipur
Tarakeshwar
Bansberia
To Jamshedpur 88 km
Arambag
Bandel
Jhilmili
BANGLADESH
BIHAR
Chandranagore
Barasat
To Jamshedpur
Howrah
Sealdah
Basirhat
Midnapore
Ulbaria
Calcutta
Kharagpur
Port Canning
To Joshipur 151 km
Belda
Diamond Harbour
SUNDERBANS
ORISSA
Contai
To Baleshwar 76 km
Digha
Gangaa Sagar
Bakkhali
New Moore I (INDIA)
N
BAY OF BENGAL
Based upon Survey of India map with the permission of the Surveyor General of India.
©GOVERNMENT OF INDIA COPYRIGHT, 1987
The territorial waters of India extend into the sea to a distance of twelve nautical miles measured from the appropriate base line.

2

The Tribal Situation in West Bengal

I

Modern West Bengal is a truncated State comprising an area of 87,676 sq. km., a legacy of British colonialism who finally left the country in 1947. The very name Bengal in the past was probably derived from a word *Bonga* - a popular Austro-Asiatic word very commonly used by the Santals, one of the major agricultural tribes of India, signifying 'holy' or 'super-natural power'. This indicates the interlaced association of an olden Austric-speaking group of the region and even today in many place-names of this State this is being reflected. The physical features of the State will appear, to a casual observer, a land with diversities, namely, snowcapped mountainous regions with sky-kissed peaks in the extreme north, terraced undulations, slowly sloping down to the south with variable gradations, mixed with alluvium and ultimately embracing the foaming and dancing bay in the southern tip, which is geographically known as 'coastal sandy region'. While the submountainous region is known as 'Tarai' that proceeds southernly as the northern plain. The south-eastern part of the region is dotted with thick and monotonous estuarine jungles, popularly known as *Sundarbans* where plenty of *Sundari (Heritiera fomes)* trees grow and shelter the famous Royal Bengal tiger along with wild animals. Of course, the major portion of this Sundarbans has now fallen in Bangladesh which was curved out of the Indian Union by the knives of the politicians and ultimately accepted mostly by many of the leaders of our country. The south-western tract has originated from the archaic rugged terrain of Chhotanagpur, evenly distributed with granite outcrops or small hillocks. Scanty jungle of dwarf *Sal (Shorea Robusta)* and other trees and plants clothed some of the surfaced lands. Of course, history retells through the availability of plenty of core stone tools belonging to the Palaeolithic period which goes as far back as to an approximation of 1,00,000 years, supplemented by chipped, ground and polished stone tools signifying the beginning of agriculture and settled human life.

On such a backdrop, we find living a good number of so called tribal communities who are popularly known as *Adivasis*, i.e. the *Bhumiputras*, the early settlers or 'autochthonese'. These groups of people have simple technology. For conceptual purposes, they speak a common language or dialect, have a common culture, are more clan-based, i.e., kin oriented or ethnocentric in temperament with less hierarchy and less economic specialisation, indicating 'mechanical solidarity' as propounded by Durikheim. The erstwhile Bengal Presidency had its headquarters at Calcutta, consisting of Provinces of Orissa-

Bihar-and a portion of Bengal of the relevant time, which is now known as Bangladesh. Even Mughal ruler Sah Suja (1639-1659) had its headquarters at Midnapur. However, the so-called Bhumiputras or the tribal group of people lived since the hoary past and had the advantage of interaction which in many cases alienated them from the one group and the other and sometimes brought many into one through blending processes of assimilation. It is also an accepted fact that the tribal groups are not permanent crystalline structure in any stage of history. What with the waves of migration of the dominant groups and what with the fear of their annihilation of the recalcitrant elements and by the viable acculturating processes, they were compelled to take shelter in the inhospitable regions which are less accessible areas, just to keep their body and soul together and keep their cultural entities. But harsh historical processes, prompted by socio-economic needs, brought many of them to a lasting assimilation scene and threw them into the arms of the broader societies around. Even so, today we find in many places distinctiveness in their cultural and pristine religious spheres a reflection though slow but steady processes of interaction in various ways, exposing them to many transformational conditions. However, they are composed of a peculiar tribal virility larded with simplicity, and also they lack the desire of possession of much material objects.

II

In point of fact, we shall deal with the tribal groups who have been Scheduled, i.e., who get the advantage of the consitutional benefits on the basis of which money is allocated for their upliftment. In this connection, it may be said that some tribals, in many cases, are found to live in distinct political boundaries or States which have been divided for administrative purposes.

In 1951, altogether 7 groups of tribal people in West Bengal were declared Scheduled and this has been mentioned in the records of the 1951 census. Subsequently, this list was further amended in pursuance of the Scheduled Castes and Scheduled Tribes Orders (Amendment) Act, 1956 when the number in West Bengal increased to 19, in respect of the Scheduled Tribes. This number was recommended by the Backward Classes Commission which was constituted by the Government of India. Again, we find changes in this figure due to reorganisation of States in 1956 when West Bengal was given some portion of Bihar. Purulia, a separate district, was formed and a corridor was provided to the northern side of West Bengal which also previously belonged to Bihar. The list was further modified and revised to some extent, bringing the total number of the tribes to 41. However, after the promulgation of the Scheduled Castes and Scheduled Tribes (Amendment) Act in 1976, the limitation of the area and the identification of the Tribes have been done and ultimately we find 38 Scheduled tribes distributed in different parts of West Bengal. Of course, there are some areas where some tribes are concentrated, but many more tribal people had to migrate long ago due to various forces of push and pull, viz., demand for tribal labour in Tea Plantation areas, the urgent requirements of the Zemindars for clearing the jungles in the Sundarbans and also to meet the demand of the Indigo Planters as also the seasonal agricultural labours (*'Namal'*, i.e., coming down to the low land) to the region where the owners of lands need them during sowing and harvesting season. Forces of urbanisation have also their share as they provide these groups some attraction for earning easy money as labourers. These have been the forces which, in the circumstantial exigencies, brought the tribals and encouraged them to form satellite villages in and around the city centres or the areas of affluence.

III

The tribal scenario of West Bengal is a bit different when we shall see their distribution in different districts of the State. But on the basis of the linguistic affinities they can be categorised into three broad groups, though almost all of them are bilingual or multi-lingual.

Table 2.1

Tribal Groups : Total Population and Linguistic Affinities

Sl. No.	*Name of the Tribes*	*Linguistic Affinities*	*Total N. of Population (1981 Census)*
1.	Asur	Austro-Asiatic	4,286
2.	Baiga	Indo-Aryan	1,606
3.	Bedia/Bediya	"	29,396
4.	Bhumij	Austro-Asiatic	233,906
5.	Bhutia	Tibeto-Burmese	40,192
6.	Birhor	Austro-Asiatic	658
7.	Birjia	"	913
8.	Chakma	Indo-Aryan	141
9.	Chero	"	1,648
10.	Chik Baraik	"	12,624
11.	Garo	Tibeto-Burman	3,206
12.	Gond	Dravidian	4,923
13.	Gorait	Indo-Aryan	2,191
14.	Hajang	"	1,035
15.	Ho	Austro-Asiatic	3,202
16.	Karmali	Indo-Aryan	1,418

17.	Kharwar	Austro-Asiatic	11,726
18.	Khond	Dravidian	639
19.	Kisan	"	5,370
20.	Kora	Indo-Aryan	96,835
21.	Korwa	"	2,493
22.	Lepcha	Tibeto-Burman	23,409
23.	Lodha/Kheria/Kharia	Austro-Asiatic	53,718
24.	Lohara/Lohra	"	23,799
25.	Magh	Tibeto-Burman	1,020
26.	Mahali	Austro-Asiatic	50,288
27.	Mahli	"	10,827
28.	Malpahariya	Dravidian	17,020
29.	Mech	Tibeto-Burman	26,959
30.	Mru	Austro-Asiatic	1,231
31.	Munda	Austro-Asiatic	230,016
32.	Nagesia	"	7,745
33.	Oraon	Dravidian	437,574
34.	Parhaiya	Austro-Asiatic	3,745
35.	Rabha	Tibeto-Burman	11,256
36.	Santal	Austro-Asiatic	1,666,610
37.	Sauria Paharia	Dravidian	4,283
38.	Savar	Austro-Asiatic	37,247

Source : Census of India 1981 : Scheduled Tribe.

But it is paradoxically true that somehow or other the Lodhas, one of the denotified tribes and now designated as a 'Primitive Tribal Group', have been bracketted with the Kherias or the Kharias. It may be due to their common claim to be identified as the *Savaras*, a 'fowling or trapping' community, who wanted to have their names enter the epic literature, wherein we find frequent mention of the name of 'Savara', a forest dwelling or marginal tribe. Of course, some Hindu influence prevails among them and this has taken deep root into their mind and culture for sharing the fascinating and dominating Hindu social system. Most of them try to fall back upon the nostalgia of their olden days of living in pleasure-roaming in the jungles, depending on their forest produce and on hunting-gathering economy. But it appears from our survey that they have a distinctive socio-cultural life; but the common forest based ecology drew them to some common pursuits and to some sort of apparent alignment.

In this connection, it may be said that the Santals are a dominating Austric-speaking people and due to their strong political organisation and stable economy from their agricultural gains, they always wear a broad grin on their faces and are not afraid of facing any situation at all times, of day and night. However, changes due to Hindu influence is noticeable among them at times when they are asserted as 'Majhis' when they give up many of their original tribal attributes through Safa *hor* movement. The Mundas have little affinity with the Santals so far as their language is concerned. But they are more Hinduised, though many of them speak in their own dialect. But their clan organisation and other aspects vary. The Mahalis are nothing but the Santals, as we find many more clan names of the Mahalis are linked with that of the Santals. This may be due to the fact that occupational specialisation involving their bamboo work has separated them from the Santals. They have become 'Mahalis' only following the caste-guild model. *Mah* means bamboo in Austric language and they specialise in the bamboo work as they crawl in caste bound social system which provide them an occupational and economic security. The associated traits of culture prompted them to accept and ultimately specialize in bamboo work. The term 'Kora' indicates 'small' or 'little'. Possibly, this group originally belonged to the great *Hor* (Santal) race and had to work as day labourer, without having sufficient agricultural land holdings. This categorised them as *Kora* which means little or 'small'. In this connection it may be said that most of the terms attributed to these groups of the so-called tribes are deliberately attributed to them by the stronger brethren and in course of time they had to accept these unhesitatingly, though in many cases they have their own term for ethnic or group identity. The Santals call themselves *Hor*, meaning 'man', whereas others are called by them as Diku, i.e. alien which possibly is the English root word for 'dacoit'. Prof. S.K. Chatterjee is of the opinion that the terms Santal has been derived from the word Samanta-Pal or the 'border guard' who live in and around the periphery of the Hindu dwelling villages. These people have to accept the term and even in our Constitution they are recognised as Santals and they assert themselves so at times for having retribalisation (Bhowmick, 1975) to merit the advantages of some Constitutional benefits. Some north-eastern tribes also are wrongly identified in different terms and this they are now found to be protesting. These terms were brought in use during the colonial rule due to their lack of understanding. For example, the 'Daflas' now assert themselves as 'Nishi', 'Mikir' as 'Arleng' etc. The very term 'Kuki' is considered to be derogatory by the so-called Kuki group of people. Nevertheless, we are concerned with the names by which they are identified and listed as 'Scheduled' during the census operations. We are to admit that many of the tribes either by alienation from the main group or forced by alien pressures, had to identify themselves with such names as prevalent then.

Though the colonial administrators recorded these facts by collecting data with little verification, they rather tried to see India with a distinctive outlook segmented vertically as well as horizontally, as the process of gathering and interpreting the facts were possibly done by a kind of monologuing process and thus have become culturally 'isolated' in the greater Indian context. But our Indian ethnographers in most cases are re-interpreting them through dialogues, getting a very clear image profile of the tribal communities who also contributed potentially to build up Indian civilization. In this case, we have to admit that Constitutional facilities, economic and political gains combinedly have accentuated the idea of distinct identity for such a categorisation.

IV

Economy of a group of people with primitive technology depends on the ecology, environment and adaptational processes which lead to cultural traits. The people have to sustain themselves by exploiting the natural resources. But in some cases, changes of economy are due to various other factors - migration to different regions and availability of new employment facilities due to changing situations. In spite of all these, we find that, the Birhors *(Bir* - jungle and *hor* - man) who live on the Bengal-Bihar border), i.e., in the undulating hills of Purulia, are not agriculturists. They are *gathering - hunting* people with their traditionalism. They used to make ropes twisting the bark of some wild trees. Their number is 165 as per our own fieldwork. Next to the Birhors, are the Lodhas, who also indulge in the same sort of economy of gathering-hunting, specially in the jungle covered areas. Their main concentration is in Midnapur district and in the adjoining jungle tracts of Mayurbhanj (Orissa) and some places of Singhbhum (Bihar). These groups have been encapsulated with the region which once provided them a bountiful natural products; hence, the old tradition continues, though we find gradual stages of their transformation while they moved to the eastern tracts of Midnapur. This might be the result of push and pull factors of better living facilities. This Lodha group of people had to bear the stigma of born-criminality. The group is again categorised as one of the major Primitive Group of people. The Kherias or Kharias, who are considered as equals with the Lodhas, as far in West Bengal concerned also live in adjoining regions of Bihar and Orissa where they are more in number. But we find them numerous in the districts of Purulia, Bankura and Midnapur. This Kharia Group, with their jungle based economy, is in the Primitive stage, and lack of communication facilities to the habitats of these people, put them more in suspension. These groups are again bracketted with the Lodhas and, as such, they enjoyed the facilities extended to the Primitive Tribal Groups. The other major Austro-Asiatic language group of people are dominated by the Santals, who are distributed in almost all the districts, of which Midnapur has the highest concentration. They are basically settled agriculturists and they subsist on plough cultivation. Of course, occasional hunting expeditions are in practice among them. The Mundas also represent a settled agriculturist group, but they move in many districts in search of better employment facilities. They are greatly Hinduised, docile and very much peaceable people. The Asura group of people were traditionally iron-smelters, but nowadays due to the changing circumstances, they engage themselves in agricultural activities. The Koras are also day labourers and agriculturists. The Mahalis are traditionally basket makers, though some of them take to agriculture in a limited way. The Oraons are basically Dravidian-speaking people, who mainly depend on plough cultivation. But some of them have accepted the job of sweeping and scavenging work while they live in the urban setting of Calcutta. In the Sundarbans, However, and also in the tea-estates, they are known as good and sincere labourers. The tribes belonging to Tibeto-Burmese language group are the Rabha, Garo, Chakma, Bhutia, Mugh, Mech, Lepcha,

Hajang and the Totos. They practise agriculture and many of them are employed in tea gardens. The Totos are very small in number (totalling-852), and prefer to be employed in gardening. They are being employed in the plantations as day labourers in the border regions of Bengal or in the impounded areas at the foot hills surrounded by the mountainous walls and the gorging streams. This group is framed in a narrow territory. A few decades ago their numbers gradually dwindled. They also belonged to one of the Primitive Tribal Groups in West Bengal and thus are enjoying the facilities extended to them.

Table 2.2
Distribution of Tribes in West Bengal

Sl. No. District	*Tribes with 1971 Population*	*Total 1971*	*Population 1981*
1. Calcutta	Oraon (167), Kora (7), Garo (59) Chakma (3), Nagesia (47), Bhutia (38), Bhumij (10), Mugh (1), Maipaharia (1), Mahali (25), Munda (248), Mech (1), Rabha (2), Lepcha (31 Lodha/Kheria (48), Santal (1,454), Hajang (22), Ho (71), others (1,973)..	2,401	4,420
2. Cooch Bihar	Oraon (214), Kora (13) Garo (898) Behar Bhutia (40), Bhumij 10, Mahali (12), Munda (943, Mech (66), Rabha (1,891), Lepcha (3),		

Sl. No.	*District*	*Tribes with 1971 Population*	*Total 1971*	*Population 1981*
		Lodha/ Kheria (248), Santal (2,880), Others (1,086).	10,611	10,105
3.	24-Parganas	Oraon (22,622), Kora (194), Garo (314), Chakma (21), Nagesia (58), Bhutia (59), Bhumij (20,004), Mugh (14), Malpaharia (138), Mahali (1,389), Munda (48,352), Mech (45), Mru (15), Rabha (105), Lepcha (44), Lodha/ Kheria (552), Santal (547), Hajang (69), Others (11,382).	137,197	189,044
4.	Jalpaiguri	Oraon (1,59,619), Kora (641), Garo (428), Nagesia (1,530), Bhutia (3,241), Bhumij (6,181), Mugh (80), Malpaharia (10,505), Mahali (24,320), Munda (71,685), Mech (10,387), Mru (30), Rabha (343), Lepcha (901), Lodha/Kheria (14,100), Santal (71,539), Hajang (47), Ho (3), Others (47,214).	428,595	491,791
5.	Darjeeling	Oraon (26,682), kaamali (715), Garo (230), Chakma (59), Chukbairik (1,544), Nagesia (855), Bhutia (30,442), Mugh (42), Malpaharia (2,443), Mahali (647), Munda (6,894), Mech		

Sl. No.	*District*	*Tribes with 1971 Population*	*Total Population 1971*	*1981*
		(253), Lepcha (13,536), Lodha/Kheria (1,744), Santal (10,335), Hajang (46), Others (12,167).	108,586	151,073
6.	Nadia	Oraon (10,470), Kora (143), Garo (158), Chakma (12), Bhumij (2,824), Mugh (5), Malpaharia (1,217), Mahali (238), Munda (5,561), Mru (532),Lepcha (2), Loha/Kheria (164), Santal (8,423), Others (1,950).	31,799	55,984
7.	West Dinajpur	Asur (611), Oraon (33,755), Karmali Dinajpur (41), Korwa (2,778), Kore (4,255), Khorwar (134), Garat (22), Garo (112), Gond (46), Chikbalrik (83), Chere (175), Parhaiya (22), Saoria Paharia (106), Birjhia (16), Bedia (96), Bhutia (7), Bhumij (706), Mugh (121), Malpaharia (6,435), Mahali (4,870), Munda (19,864), Mech (12), Rabha (1), Lepcha (1,257), Savar (501), Santal (1,30,473), Hajang (41), Ho (193), Others (14,420).	221,317	260,160

Sl. No. District	Tribes with 1971 Population	Total 1971	Population 1981
8. Purulia	Oraon (4,208), Karmali (53), Kisan (3), Korwa (444), Kora (13,343), Garet (459), Paharia (2), Saoria Paharia (158), Bedis (3,243), Bhumij (52,989), Malpaharia (231), Mahli (998), Mahali (18), Munda (10,609), Lepcha (6), Lodha/Kheria (1,899)	313,792	348,475
9. Bardhaman	Oraon (2,819), Kora (19,530), Garo (352), Chakma (1), Bhutis (3), Bhumij (1,320), Mugh (285), Malpaharia (549), Mahali (1,550), Munda (2,956), Lepcha (6), Lodha/Kheria (22), Santal (180,280), Hajang (7), Ho (13), Other (18,871).	228,605	278,191
10. Bankura	Oraon (2,982), Kora (13,103), Bhumij (24,029), Mahali (1,101), Munda (4,441), Rabha (1), Lodha/Kheria (141), Santal (157,806), Others (1,208).	208,735	250,598
11. Birbhum	Oraon (2,281), Kora (10,598), Chakma (3), Bhumij (31), Mugh (2,419), Malpaharia (1,463), Mahali (3,181), Munda (56), Lodha/Kheria (28), Santal		

Sl. No.	*District*	*Tribes with 1971 Population*	*Total 1971*	*Population 1981*
		(104,722), Ho (133), Others (335).	125,250	145,133
12.	Malda	Oraon 10,325), Kora (8,378), Chakma (2,828), Bhutia (3), Bhumij (142), Malpaharia (4,654), Mahali (2,756), Munda (5,264), Lodha / Kheria (1,567), Santal (90,285), Others (4,310).	130,715	153,300
13.	Midnapur	Oraon (3,499), Kora (11,640), Garo (30), Bhutia (15), Bhumij (5,752), Mugh (107), Malpaharia (22), Mahali (6,479), Munda (18,418), Mech (64), Mru (96), Rabha (117), Lepcha (23), Lodha / Kheria (18,434), Santal (286,010), Ho (185), Others (40,295)	442,963	538,877
14.	Murshidabad	Oraon (3,371), Kora (896), Garo (12), Bhutia (3), Mugh (4), Malpaharia (334), Mahali (370), Munda (837), Lepcha (4), Lodha / Kheria (93), Santal (28,220), Ho (5), Others (1,778.)	38,947	45,302
15.	Howrah	Oraon (458), Kora (57), Garo (1), Chikbairik (4), Bhutia (5), Bhumij (83), Mugh (180), Malpaharia (6),		

Sl. No.	District	Tribes with 1971 Population	Total 1971	Population 1981
		Mahali (22), Munda (884), Mech (32), Lepcha (2), Lodha/Kheria (47), Santal (242), Hajang (3), Ho (29), Others (312).	3,364	7,280
16.	Hooghly	Oraon (5,431), Kora (7,005), Garo (51), Bhutia (54), Bhumij (4,511), Mugh (1), Mahali (268), Munda (1,689), Mru (149), Lepcha (16), Lodha/Kheria (2,646), Santal (75,132), Hajang (9), Ho (11), Others (5,033).	100,084	141,047

Source : *Paschim Banger Adivasi Nirdesika,* Das and Mukhopadhyay (1977 : 60-62).

V

With regard to the social life of all the tribal groups, there are some basic uniformities. Almost all of them assert themselves to their own traditional names that are known to all. There is a little scope for inter-tribe marriages, except in rare cases at the tea estates. All these tribes have clan organisations. The Mundas in the district of Midnapur show a greater division of the tribes into *Bansha* (lineage) and *Patabhai* or sub-lineage. There are clans and almost all the clans have their respective totems, which are considered to be the identifying institutions and these clan-brotherhood restrict marriages among themselves. The totemic object is either respected or is regarded as taboo for eating or consuming, if it becomes an indispensable element of food item. All the tribal groups are patriarchate in nature, i.e. agreeing to descent, inheritance, authoritative,residential etc. all the time in the male lines, whereas the matriarchate Garo and the Rabha constitute as a very insignificant tribe in West Bengal. Their concentration is on the north-eastern tract of this country. Strong traditional social and political organisation as once it was a binding and controlling force, but due to spread of modern education and involvement of the people in modern politics, the Political Organisation has become weak. But in respect of marriage or other traditional cases of violation, this political organisation appears to tackle the situation properly with an imbibed idea of ethnocentricism. In spite of religiosity, almost all the tribal groups have their traditional deities and spirits, i.e., they have a world of the supernaturals which controls the destiny of the people. There are the Supreme god and other deities of minor nature as well as the tutelary village deities in charge of the welfare of the village, either by driving away the evil spirits or by mitigarting the supposed wrath of the gods and goddesses. The Santals strongly believe in witchcraft which is pupularly known as *Daini-Vidya*. The heartless killing of the witches as per their tradition with the help of the *Jan-guru* (who can allegedly see through the unseen evil acts by practising occultism and suggest remedial measures) is very common among them. Even these beliefs are so deeprooted that people cannot think without this. The Lodhas have also a similar concept of *Yugini*, who is supposed to spread the germ-cells of epidemic diseases. Modern education, employment in white-collar jobs and the changing scenario of these people, have some effect on the religiosity of the tribal people. Examples of conversions to other religious faiths are there among many tribals, specially to Christianity and thus many tribal people have a changing belief system now. The members of a Kharia tribe showed in special situations a very limited number of conversion cases to Islam, particularly in Midnapur district. In spite of all the amazing conglomeration of traditions, beliefs, formal rituals and practices, the tribal people remained as a conceptual model of traditionalism and all these taken together constitute and revitalise this group. This traditionalism has been handed down to them by their ancestors from generation to generation. In order to fight out the disasters and unknown evil forces of supernaturalism, many formalities in the shape of taboos, restrictions, prayers, chanting of hymns are in use to placate and pacify the deities all around them, to achieve a secured and undisturbed life and living. All these procedures, according to their tradition, can avert the occurrence of misfortune and bring success and prosperity in their life. Thus, we find worships, sacrifices and other forms of prayer to appease the displeasure of all the angry spirits who are believed to bring about illness, drought, mischance and calamities of various nature. But, in the changing situation, this sort of traditionalism has a very little place and in many places they are to adjust themselves with the changing situation of the world.

3

Cultural Profile of the Primitive Tribal Groups

I

People living at different physical setting that is differentiated by climatic conditions, vegetable cover and topography, no doubt practice different economic activities attuned to their social system which can be distinguished between one another. At the same time, bigger social environment, i.e., the influences of other ethnic groups also have an impact on the life-style of the given people. Naturally, therefore, culture of such a population has intimate relationships with the local geography in moulding the material culture of the area. Social environment can also reshape the social organisations and also the awe-inspiring physical backdrop. Unsolved problems which are beyond their calculations and understanding are attributed to some supernatural phenomena and thus a world of supernaturalism constellate around them having limitless limitations. In this way, distinctive cultural traits are brought into play. As a result, we find one group of people are differing from the other, though in many cases common geography or physical background sustain them for the sake of uniformity of a culture. People with less amount of isolation, i.e., having more interaction and communication facilities are found to change this life-style. In spite of all this compelling situations, we find how far these adaptive forces are operating in tune with the prevailing cultural processes among the people. Even if we offer them an alternative better way of life, either by supplementing or by complementing the context, we shall have to consider seriously about the physical background - the available resources, technology, their adaptive mechanism and the existing world view of the people. Along with this we will have to take into account the population structure, family size and other aspects of culture, just to have a clearer background of the population along with the existing historical forces which are operating on the life-style of the people. With this backdrop, an attempt has been made to portray the cultural profile of the primitive tribal groups of West Bengal and to diagnose the various forces operating in their cultural life when many more deliberate attempts are being made to change their life and living to a better one. Of course, until the world view and the perception level are not changed and a strong desire to have a better life generates through socialisation, interaction and other articulative processes, the change will not be successfully achieved. As a result, such a situation should be given priority before examining the nature of welfare among the group of people under survey.

II

The Totos are one of the Primitive Tribal Groups in West Bengal and they live on the northern border of our State under Madarihat Police Station of Jalpaiguri district. The village, popularly known as Totopara, is situated on slope of the hill known as Tading. Its height is about 750 ft. to 1,500 ft. above the sea level. the north-western boundary of the village is guarded by hills, whereas on the eastern side flows the gurgling Torsa and the south-western region is bathed in a small rivulet, known as Hauri. The landscape beckons a casual visitor who will find that a sprawling forest is in existence on the backdrop of lateritic undulations on the western bank of the Hauri, which has grown deep with growth of thick vegetal cover that shelters many wild animals. Black strip of metalled road zigzag through barren and rocky land punctuated by green patches at some places and ultimately the village of the Toto can be communicated by an unmetalled road of about 5 km., when regular bus service is in operation, through Madarihat. As light appears, the entire area vibrates with work of the people both the Totos and the other who struggle hard for their existence but as night falls absolute calm descends on the slope. History has it that for a pretty long time this region was under the control of the Bhutanese and ultimately the then British Government ceded it to India, after the Bhutan War in 1865. However, the British Government passed an Act, viz., Bhutan Duars Act in 1868 to assume full control of the area. The entire Totopara area is about 315 sq. miles. Mr. Sander, sometime in 1889-94, kept the place as *reserved* for the small group of these people.

Though concentration of the Totos is found at one place, some conjectural history speculates that they might have been distributed in the western Duars also. Their old settlements have been traced at the bank of the Teesta, which indicated strong association with the place in the part, particularly because of the place names that still exist here. Totogaon in Malbazar, Totopara at Dhupguri, Totopara in Alipur Duars and also Totopara in Falakata suggest the one time habitation sites of the Totos who might have migrated to the unhealthy hill slope only to eke out existence finding adversities here and there. Probably, owing to political onslaughts and organised attacks of the Bhutanese during the previous-centuries, this tribe moved out of this place and ultimately took shelter in this forest enclave, where greater discomforts haunted them constantly in the form of unhealthy living conditions and attack of diseases, as also continuous indebtedness to the money lending sharks. Though they are a small sized tribe, yet regular census taken on them gives the following figures :-

Table 3.1
Population

Year		*Households*	*Population*
1901	Census Operation	35	171
1911	"	60	255
1921	"	80	271
1931	"	-	321
1941	"	-	321
1951	"	68	395
1961	"	109	616
1962	I.S.I.	88	650
1971	Census Operation	95	675
1979	C.R.I.	123	-
1981	Census Operation	137	761
1989	Our Survey	163	852

Total population is 808, i.e. 54.41% and belong to various communities grabbing the land once recorded for Totos. (Das : 1969, Dhali : 1987) and some others who wrote sporadically on this little known tribe. The Totos are distributed in 6 hamlets bearing distinct names of each, and now a good number of the Nepalese encroached upon their Lands in different ways when the reservation order was withdrawn. The conjectural history of the Totos revealed that about eight generations earlier the group of people roamed about collecting various medicinal herbs and animal bones, and also searched for core gold and copper in and around the vicinity. They used to exchange all their collections for various food articles from the settled traders and the neighbours living in different places. The 1961 census records 109 households of this tribe with a total population of 616 (423 male and 193 female). However, Sanyal (1947, 1955, 1958) explored the tribe in detail and subsequently the Cultural Research Institute, Government of West Bengal studied them systematically.

The dwelling hut of the Totos consists of a small room with a running verandah and in most cases the huts are propped up on bamboo poles. Spilt bamboo pieces are woven together and these make their walls. Some steps are constructed with solid wood blocks. All their household implements are kept in the room and their domestic animals, viz., pigs etc. accommodated beneath the floor; all this goes to show that the Totos are a very impoverished set of people and are of unsound economy. Males have their body strong and stout but flat chested women amidst many giggles and exclamations, with their blouses having fitting arm-band, with prominent Mongoloid features, remain very unclean, which results in various skin diseases. Most of the days in the year, they consume maize and pulses which are available from the local market and also various green vegetables that are collected from the locality. They eat beef (carrion), pork, venison and flesh of many other animals. They prepare leaf-plates for their eating purposes. They also brew some kind of beer out of *Marua* and consume it in abundance.

Their economic activities are punctuated with the seasonal variations. They are mainly agriculturists, but the topography of the place does not allow them to carry on a systematic agricultural pursuit. Yet we find to cultivate vegetables, fruits, arecanuts, cotton, bambo, ginger and turmeric on a small scale. There are shops scattered here and there and a weekly market has been started, since 1978.

Table 3.2

Population Structure

Age Group	*0-14*		*15-29*		*30-40*		*45-59*		*60 & above*		*Total*
	M	*F*	*M*	*F*	*M*	*F*	*M*	*F*	*M*	*F*	
	202	183	144	136	41	42	45	43	4	12	852

The social structure of the Toto indicates that they have clans and all these clans are exogamous. The clans are 13 in number. Basically, they are a monogamous tribe. A family is the smallest social unit and the size of the family indicates how much a family needs for its smooth running.

Many rituals are observed by them in their life-style. The supernatural spirits in the form of deities, gods, goddesses etc. The chief deity, according to them is Mahakal. Worship, propitiation and sacrifices are held to appease the spirits and to gain their favour. Festivals and merri-making formalities take place during the celebration of worships etc.

Table 3.3

Family Size

Total No. of Family	*Small (1-3 members)*	*Medium (4-6 members)*	*Large (7-above)*
No. 163	40	73	50
%	(24.52%)	(44.11%)	(30.67%)

The Totos have a village council to deal with the various problems and some office-bearers are chosen to do this job. The posts of the village priest, i.e., Kaji and Mondal, the Secular Chief are hereditary. However, these docile apparently happy people with a sunny disposition have still numerous signs of poverty and difficulties writ large on their faces, though they have never a word of complain against anybody rather seem to forge more friendships than to raise animosity on their normal trek. Various welfare measures were taken from time to time morass. Finally, one welfare centre was started at Totopara, in 1951. Besides, some voluntary organisations were found to work among these hapless people for their overall development. A voluntary organisation named *Bharat Mahajati Mandali* was set up with Government grant of the State for this purpose and later the Lutheran World Service devoted themselves through many welfare schemes. These have been discussed threadbare in various chapters in this volume.

There are many indications of developmental activities, namely, (a primary and upto Class-VIII standard school), teachers' quarters, ashram hostels, staff quarters and a nice bungalow of the T.W. Department, a guest house to accommodate the outsiders have been constructed recently. Some measures of welfare in various other ways can also be noticed if the local people be examined closely. In this connection, it may be noted here that in Totopara about 800 outsiders have encroached upto 592.85 acres of land. The remaining 1051.31 acres of land is full of jungle and grass-lands with many venerated felines, and this is said to have been unauthorisedly occupied by the Forest Department. The Totos only possess 347.43 acres of land.

III

The Birhors are another Primitive Tribal Group in West Bengal mainly concentrated in the State of Bihar and rolling from the terrain to the adjoining place of West Bengal; i.e., Purulia (a newly constituted district after the State Reorganisation in 1956). They are an Austric-speaking people. The name of 'Birhor' is supposed to have been derived from *Bir* - jungle and *Hor* - man, i.e., the man who lives in the jungle. We get an elaborate description of these people from the book of S.C. Roy (1925), who described their life-style and other details of their socio-economic structures. Ray, at the beginning, elaborated the notes and memoranda from various records. Somebody described then as follows (Dalton : 1872).

> They are a small, dirty, miserable looking race, who have the credit of devouring their parents and when I talked to them with it, they did not deny that such a custom had once obtained among them.

Roy told about them (Roy:1925) in the following terms::

> They wander about or settle down for a time in small groups of three or four to get about their family earning - a precious subsistence by hunting deer and other animals and fowls and snaring monkeys, by collecting *Chop (Banhinia Scandena)* and making them into ropes for barter or sale in the nearest villages or markets and by gather bee-wax and honey when available.

Originally, one section of them basically is wanderer and is known as *Uthlus* or *Bhulias*, whereas the more or less settled group is known as *Jaghis* or *Thanias*. They generally live in their traditional small settlements of conical type of huts *(Kumbo)* prepared out of grass and creepers and the settlement is known as *Tanda*. They are basically a gathering-hunting group and they wander around the sources of food stuffs. They have a well organised hunting group and their catches are distributed equally, with a little extra quantity for the leader. Naturally, their household implements consist of various snares, bows and arrows, and slings etc. along with some pots and pans.

They have a good number of totemic clans and Roy puts them to about 37 in number. Their marriages take place outside the clan. There are formalities, rites and rituals associated with such marriages. S.C. Roy indicated the existence of the practice of dormitory living, but these have fallen into disuse now.

They in this tract of border Bengal situated at the foot of the tree crowned Ayodhya hill live in three villages which have been studied by the scribe, while examining the evaluation results of the welfare programme. Distant images appear to be deceptive but while scrutinising in detail the signs of abject poverty will confirm the condition which made them categorised as PTG. They are docile, defenceless without good-water. Many conditions made them suspicious to the other people specially the Government officers or the Panchayat leaders. The population structure of the three villages inhabited by the Birhors has been reflected in Table 3.4.

Table 3.4
Population Structure

Village	AGE GROUP										Total
	0-14		15-29		30-44		45-59		60 & above		
	M	F	M	F	M	F	M	F	M	F	
1. Bhup-atipalli 2. Bararia 3. Baridi	39	23	25	20	11	12	16	17	2	-	165

Family size of the Birhor has been relfected in Table 3.5.

Table 3.5
Family Size

Total No. of Family	Small (1-3 members)	Medium (4-6 members)	Large (7-above)
47 (100%)	26 (55.3%)	19 (40.4%)	2 ($.3%)

Again, the size of a Birhor family is estimated on the basis of the number of persons in the family. It is true that gathering-hunting community cannot sustain big sized families where various activities are in demand for maintaining their day to day existence.

Like many other communities, they also believe in the presence of various spirits and supernatural elements which control the destiny of the people. *Sing Bonga* is regarded by the Birhors as their supreme deity. He is supposed to be a benevolent god. Once in a year, he is worshipped. *Chando Bonga* may be regarded as another benevolent deity. There is a concept that *Veer* or *Hero* who is regarded as the controlling deity in different situations.

The Birhors categorise two types of ancestral spirits- *Hapram* and *Churgin*. Animal is sacrificed at the time of their worships. All the malevolent spirits are categorised as 'Churgin'. It also includes spirits of the dead. The Birhors identify about 8 such spirits in their pantheon.

Welfare activities were taken long back and a rehabilitation colony was started long ago when Late Bhupati Mazumdar was the Minister-in-charge of Tribal Welfare. In truest sense, economic needs are exacerbated by the fact that when no land is available and the people do not know cultivation process besides fields around them are arid and merciless. Bhupatipalli, a rehabilitated spot where available resources are considered to be better and, as such they were brought close to the neighbouring villages and put in a group cutting across the tribal coyness and ethnocentric gestures. However, details of the welfare projects have been discussed on the basis of the items meant for them when they were included in the 'Primitive Tribal Group' to examine the nature of benefits accrued out of the programmes initiated by the Government even through the Panchayat machineries.

IV

The Lodhas are considered to be one of the Primitive Tribal Groups in West Bengal. Previously, they were known as a 'Criminal Tribe' till the revocation of the Criminal Tribes Act in 1952. They are mainly concentrated in the jungle-covered region of western Midnapur and even to some extent in the adjoining areas of Mayurbhanj (Orissa) and Singhbhum (Bihar). The 1951 Census recorded their numbers as 8,346 but now the total number is about 26,000 in Midnapur alone. This may be due to the stigma of criminality they bear which conpelled them not to be identified as 'Lodha' in the past and suffer.

The very term 'Lodha' is possibly derived from the word 'Lubdhaka' which means 'trapper' or `fowler'. Actually, they are a gathering-hunting community. Once they depended on the bounty of forests. Collection of jungle produce, edible roots and tubers, small games etc. was their main occupation, but after the enactment of the "Permanent Settlement Act" (1793) by the then British administration, the entire region of forests was given to the landlords and in this way their right over the forest produce was set at naught; ultimately, they became paupers from the level of poverty. Helpless as they are, they were flooded with all sorts of criminal activities, true or imaginary. Goaded by the pangs of hunger and tyranny of the rich receivers belonging to varied political parties, the Lodhas practically had no other alternative than to fall back upon for a living. Territorial and economic displacement made them real pagans. The economically displaced Lodhas could not adapt themselves to the changing situation and ultimately they were further driven to a precarious existence. The growing needs of their expanding family fixed them in a frame of narrow territory in which they could not meet their dire needs with small and irregular income. Unending frustration and lack of self-confidence brought in its train a perpetual stagnation in their collective life which subsequently turned them into inveterate criminals with every thrust of waves of the changing circumstances. Thus, criminality cut a deep gorge and these hapless people had to role down helplessly in it.

But, nowadays, we find some distinctiveness in the group. Some of those who live mainly on the southern bank of the river Subarnarekha, including the areas in Jhargram and Jamboni Police Stations have categorised themselves as 'Jungle Lodhas', whereas the other section, who possibly migrated to the eastern tract, have been gradually engaging themselves as agriculturists and taking other jobs. But the group, as a whole, has a very distinctive characteristic - they are stout and strong, ever disbelieving the alien group as they are being cheated and exploited by the latter all the time, they are basically lazy and take to sharp practices, speak in distorted local Bengali dialect with an admixture of Austric words.

Their main economy is gathering-hunting, collection of honey and foggots, *tusser cocoons* or *gooty*, from the jungles and also edible roots and tubers and small games from there. They sell their collections to the local people at a throw away price and purchase some of their essential food articles in exchange. Regarding their equipments, bows and arrows, digging sticks or axes are their main items or equipment. They also hunt various poisonous and non-poisonous snakes, lizards, the skins of which are sold to local people at a high price.

In the jungle areas, practically most of the people live in single-room huts having no shutters to the door. The comparatively affluent people have mud-built and four-sloped houses with doors and shutters. The number of their household utensils are very few. Even clothings are not a plenty and they are shabby and ugly to look at except the feed who are favoured in many ways. Regarding their economic activities, as stated earlier those who live near to the jungles, collect fire wood, put them in bundles and sell them to the nearest market or locality. They spend their sale proceeds on food and other essential articles. Sometime they are found to work as wage-earners, working in the field of others or in road construction work or some such activities. They grapple with their abject poverty year in and year out in two stages :-

(a) a period of feast and

(b) period of fast.

After the rainy season, they get some employment opportunities and they also collect various fruits, water lily, molusca and they eat sell these in the market, but after March nothing is available. They then fall on thin times and face a near-famine condition.

Table 3.6

Population Structure

Age Group	*0-14*		*15-29*		*30-44*		*45-59*		*60 & above*		*Total*
	M	*F*	*M*	*F*	*M*	*F*	*M*	*F*	*M*	*F*	
	244	261	188	239	95	925	107	132	6	9	1,406

A good number of children, below the age of 14 are found to be employed in some houses as *Bagal*, tenderer of grazing cattle. They are very reluctant to go to the schools, though nearby schools are available. Early marriage is in vogue, but divorce and remarriage or *Sanga* are also commonly found in the Lodha villages.

Table 3.7

Family Size

Total No. of Family	*Small (1-3 members)*	*Medium (4-6 members)*	*Large (7-above members)*
288 (100%)	86 (29.86%)	158 (54.86%)	44 (15.28%)

Table 3.7 indicates the nature of family as found in the Lodha society. Simple families are very common, even old parents have to stay in lonely condition, as the grown up offsprings could not afford to feed them.

The Lodhas have elaborate clan organisations, which are totemic and number nine. Almost all the clans have their respective totems. Marriage in the same clan is strictly forbidden, but inter-tribe marriages are found in a few cases where non-Lodhas became interested in keeping a Lodha concubine.

The Lodhas have an elaborate political organisation. The traditional village Panchayat has to look after the problems of the village when a complaint is lodged. But nowadays due to the presence of different political parties the traditional Panchayats have been to lose their importance and power. The Head of the political organisation is known as Mukhia. He has an assistant called Dakua, who is nothing but the bailiff or village messenger. In the olden days, the village political organisation had tremendous role to play in controlling the village affairs. But these days it is going to fade out.

The Lodhas believe in the mysterious spirits, i.e., gods and goddesses, evil spirits etc. There are also village tutelary deities - 'Baram' or 'Garam'. A very old tree is considered to be the seat of 'Baram'. For an elaborate ritual performance, there are village priests to help. They are called Deheris and their assistant is called Talia. These posts are hereditary. Worships are associated with animal sacrifice accompanied with songs and dances by way of celebration. In all their songs, there are vibrations of Hindu culture. The language of these songs is distorted Bengali.

As the Lodhas wear the stigma of criminality, many people do not trust them wholly. And there were a good number of inter-tribe hostilities in the past which took a heavy toll of Lodha lives. Naturally, a new mentality has to be grown to tackle this problem and bring a stable solution for the problem. As the Lodhas were considered a criminal tribe, they were straight-jacketted with various restrictions and control orders. But still their habit of criminality persists as the administrators failed to tackle their problems and the politicians failed to deal with them sympathetically rather they utilise for political game.

Before they were listed as a Scheduled tribe they were under the control of the Home (Police) Department. Attempts were then made fitfully to build up a model colony for them to enable them to turn over a new leaf in life and also make them agriculture minded in order to foster a sense of belonging among them. But such attempts to bring them to the fold of the bigger society still remain a far cry. Mass killing of the Lodhas was a common feature in the past. In consideration of their living conditions, some welfare work has initiated by the Home (Police) Department and subsequently they became entitled to enjoy the benefits of many such projects, just to bolster up their economic base. There are some voluntary organisations also which have involved themselves in this work among the Lodhas. The results of the projects have not, however, been as satisfactory as one desires. It is a fact that they require some psycho-emotional adjustments through socialisation processes and mutual interactions. They have some pseudo-friends in the form of receiver of stolen property who want to exploit them and keep the pot of criminality boiling. On many occasions when the neighbouring communities were greatly incensed against their recurring criminal activities which had cost them their lives. Some of them were mercilessly beaten and maimed. Mass killing of the Lodhas took a different turn when their humble huts were set on fire, for they were lift with nothing to fall back upon in life.

Table 3.8

Mass-killing of the Lodha

Year	*Location*	*No. of Lodha Victims*	*Groups blamed to be responsible*
1961	Dhanghari/ Dhansola PS Binpur	2 killed, (entire village was set on fire)	Santal, Mahato, Bhumij

1968	Jhargram PS	5 killed, (18 villages were set on fire)	Santal
1979	Patina, Nayagram PS	19 killed, and a few deformed and mutilated.	About 4,000 people of all tribes and castes.
1981	Ganua, PS Narayangarh	8 killed and 12 deformed and mutilated.	Local people of all castes.
1982	Nunmungeria PS Jhargram	2 and a few deformed and mutilated.	Local people/ Santal.
1982	Soro, Bagjhapa Chandri, Chakna	6 killed	Local people.
1982	Keshiary and Kharagpur Pingla	4 killed many deformed and mutilated.	Local people.

However, still this feeling is continuing, though a good number of the Lodhas are educated and have the opportunity of mixing with the bigger society to overcome the age-old stigma of criminality.

V

A good number of the Kharias have been bracketted with the Lodhas and, as such, the benefits earmarked for the PTG (Primitive Tribal Group). Originally the Kharias live in the hilly and forest clad areas of West Bengal, Bihar and Orissa. Although the Kharias in these three States are supposed to comprise as single tribe, there are cultural differences. So far in West Bengal the Kharias are mostly concentrated in the districts of Purulia, Bankura and Midnapur. Slow conversion to Islam among them has been noticed when this group gradually migrated to the eastern tract of Midnapur and came in touch with Islam. But many of their jungle habits, which related to the past dwelling in forests, still linger, e.g. killing of animal by hunting or using telescopic spears, catching snakes and playing with them, using palm leaf mats etc. They are an Austric speaking people. However, leaving aside all these, we find that the Kharias are one of the 'Primitive Tribal Groups' and therefore are getting the benefits of Welfare given by the Government. Roy and Roy (1937) wrote an elaborate ethnographic account of these people. These authors have given vivid account and Prof. T.C. Das described the Kharias of Dhalbhum and portrayed their colourful socio-economic life. In West Bengal, their number runs to about 8,000. Kharia life is inextricately related to the forest ecosystem. They live in small villages situated in accessible forest tracts. Their adaptation to the environment is direct and simple. Their level of technology is just enough to cope with their gathering economy. In the past they led a life of 'natural man' in the blissful environment along with bounty of nature they used to consider themselves as the masters of the forest tract they inhabited and as such many more clan names are associated with the territory. In the past their forest habitat sustained them as there was less pressure on forest, and forest management rules were liberal. But with the development of the forest policy and rise of commercial forestry, restriction on the use of forest, including collection of produce, has been progressively brought about. The traditional rights on their forest ecosystem have been squeezed and consequently their plight and tribulations have increased. However, the Kharia tribe is divided into three distinct divisions : viz. Pahari or Erenga Kharia, Dhelki Kharia, and Dudh Kharia. However, population structure of the Kharias appears as follows :

Table 3.9

Population Structure with Age Group

Age Group	*0-14*		*15-29*		*30-44*		*45-59*		*60 & above*		*Total*
	M	*F*	*M*	*F*	*M*	*F*	*M*	*F*	*M*	*F*	
	201	170	214	138	85	89	87	84	6	12	1,086

Naturally, there might be differnces in their life styles, inasmuch as apparently there are physical differences among these people. It is believed that the 'Hill Kharias' have Cobra or *Nag* as their clan. Some of them of course have *Saluk* (water lily) as their clan or totem. Besides, Roy and Roy (1937) describe that six important clans are dominant among the Kharias. Among them marriage takes place outside their clan. Again, the Dhelki Kharia's elaborate organisation is based on totems and the clan members never injure or kill or consume the totem object even when it becomes an important food item of the group. There are various way of finding mates among them.

Family is the smallest unit among the Kharias, Table 3.10 reflects the size of the family.

Table 3.10

Family Size

Total No. of Family	*Small (1-3 members)*	*Medium (4-6 members)*	*Large (7 & above members)*
216 (99.99%)	9 (4.16%)	173 (80.09%)	34 (15.74%)

The economic activities of the Kharias of Purulia have been described in detail (Sinha : 1984). It is true that most of them indulge in gathering and foraging economy, though these vary as per seasonal vagaries. Hunting of small games, collecting and selling of honey, selling a little of their handicrafts consisting of broomsticks or fish-traps and, lastly, serving as day labourers in many places are the important avocations of their life. Due to rapid deforestation, this group had to be practically deprived of many of their rights and privileges and, as such, had to co-exist without a demur with hunger and starvation. To reach many Kharia villages specially in Purulia, Bankura and Midnapur, there is no road, visitor has to climb slowly through the almost deforested *dungris* i.e. hillocks. Economic pressures and migratory life-style generally push them from their idle landscape and some potential workforce try to chase new job popularly known as *Namal*-'coming down' to chase the job of agricultural labour and come back before *Paush Sankranti* (Mid-January). Feeling hemmed in and as such this new adventure continues.

In spite of all these, they believe in the existence of many mysterious spirits, some of whom are benevolent and some are malevolent. They consider, the sun, the moon and the natural calamities as the attributes of some mysterious power to them. The hills of the locality are considered to be the abodes of gods and goddesses. They have an elaborate rituals and they worship gods and goddesses generally with the help of the village priests. There are many other festivals related to the seasons. Besides, there are some other local and endemic festivities. Ancestors' spirits are worshipped by them with a view to seek the blessings of the ancestors' manes for the welfare of the family. The priest is known locally as *Laya* and the post is hereditary. Many more festivals are performed when the people assemble with their musical instruments.

The Kharias have the traditional village Panchayat to deal with problems of their life. All the elderly persons are considered to be its valid members. The head of the organisation is designated as *Kale* or *Baigo*. But, nowadays the Panchayat is not properly functioning due to rapid and thrustful politicisation in the state.

VI

Now, it is important to note here that whenever any welfare work is to be done for a given community, the person in charge of translating various measures, must know in detail the cultural background of the people concerned, i.e., the anatomy of the society. Besides, he should know the nature of relationships of other neighbouring ethnic groups with that of the group in question, which has regular socio-economic interaction. Again, the region or the people where the people live should be considered critically while framing the welfare schemes. Development through systematic welfare activities, social engineering with social choice. It is to be remembered all the time that the region or the area moulds the behavour pattern of the people.

The Totos are a group of people who live in unhealthy, infertile hill slopes with less interaction outside. But certain factors arose when they were pushed into the narrower environment as the outsiders encroached upon their privileges. Besides ill health, sickness, unclean habits have put them in a more precarious condition which threatened them all the while. Naturally, education, modern health and hygienic measures are the crying needs of the hour for them, just to make them shake off their old habits. Infrastructures should be well thought out for them and at the Totopara the Missionary approach and the Government assistance that have been ushered in after the Independence is to be galvanised from time to time as these are *sine-qua non* for the Totos. The Birhors are gathering-hunting people they live near Bihar border in the slopes of the Ayodhya hills just in small sleepy villages. But their acquaintance with the outside world is less and they are doused with old ideas which are difficult to remove. To rehabilitate them in a congenial surrounding and to try to ward off all these psycho-social conditions are to be reviewed and the nature of adjustments with the modern thoughts and ideas should be considered according to the needs of the welfare measures.

Next comes the Lodhas. Though they are spread over a big area of different background, as well as a result of migration from the western jungle portions to eastern region, they had to face new environs with different ethnic groups as well as profession. As the Lodhas were compelled to live in hunger for years together, their survival strategy differs. In addition, they are being stigmatised as criminals, which path no doubt they had to tread for having no other alternative way to keep their body and soul together. This compelling situation created in them a strong bent of mind and angularities in their life-style, the impact of which changed their action pattern and outlook. Disillusionment and deprivation were all around them and they had to surrender for their survival losing many of their virtues and potentialities. Ultimately, they became inveterate criminals. They could not believe their neighbours, as they perennially cheated by the receivers while receiving their stolen properties at much the less amount of their value. Under such circumstances, planning of welfare programmes for them requires special consideration, as it requires constant socialisation and sympathetic consideration to tackle the psycho-emotional aspect. Through systematic articulation with the middle class norm, creating islands of development of hope, which can be attracted by them automatically.

The Kharias are also a tribe and have occasional anti-social activities not stigmatised in a group, but they operate only in specific areas. They are confined to an unhealthy and infertile terrain when the march of civilisation proceeded in other places more progressively, so their development needs different approach.

Now, it is to be observed how the various welfare measures started by the Government or by the voluntary organisations are being done ever finds the Independence and to see the nature of responses of the recipients. With all this background and forethought, we will have to examine the nature of benefits bestowed by the Central Government money since 1980-81 as these groups of people were considered as a Primitive Tribal Group. In Eighth Plan Period (1990-1995 : Ministry of Welfare, Tribal Development) the name of the Kharias has been dropped off from the list as the Lodha and the Kharias are distinct tribal groups.

4

Welfare Through Plans and Projects

I

It is a matter of common knowledge that the term 'tribe' (Scheduled) is attributable to many groups of people who have distinct socio-cultural life on the basis of which they can be differentiated. Besides physical geography of the region, various ethnic influence and the nature of political overtures have tremendous impact on the life-style of the people and thus a transformation process has been operating leading either to integrate them with bigger society in and around or to be identified as an exclusive isolated beings insulated with strong forces of ethnocentricism. History tells us that during the Hindu period most of the tribals of the mainland of India began to articulate with the regional Hinduism which is very very flexible indeed in nature and these have been pronounced at varied degrees. We also find an integrating undercurrent of force operating among them.

In West Bengal, the Lodhas or the Kharias/Kherias who assert themselves as 'Savaras', they pronounced as Sabbar, i.e., 'trapper or fowler', are a forest dwelling community mentioned in the Puranic literature. Even among the life of the Birhors, many more Hindu ideas and customs are reflected where influence of regional Hinduism are dominant. Naturally, a good number of tribals in different parts of this country is also known as 'Savara'—the name mentioned in ancient literatures. In this way, their identity has been pronounced at various stages of Hindu culture, which ultimately strengthened the base of Indian civilisation. Many more deities of the Hindus are even considered as the deities of the tribals. We find umpteen common deities indicating a slow but steady articulation with the Hindu society that has been forged minimising the gulf between the two. However, during the Moghul rule, the tribals became exposed to a section of administrators and quite a number of tribal concentrated areas were penetrated into by them. This allowed them to be exploited by the alien hands and a simmering discontent began to spew. This pent up feeling of annoyance ultimately gave vent to a series of insurrections and agitations at different places of India at varied degrees in the initial stage of the British penetration. Again, the British rulers thought it proper to encroach upon many of the tribal lands with some vested interest and the tribals were driven to the extreme point of exploitation. The British administration vindicated the cause of their supporter, even illegally, and in all matters, fair or fowl, their henchmen were screened against the tribal onslaughts. All this errupted like a volcano and the lava of agitations struck terror into the mind of the sinful administrators. In this context, the statement of J.H. Hutton is significant. [From Dhebar Commission Report (1961)]:

> ...far from being immediate benefit, to the primitive tribes, the establishment of British Rule in India did much more harm.

However, the British policy of isolation put the tribes into the hands of zemindars, landlords, contractors and money-lenders. They practically began to suck the life-hood of these simple, simpletons and nature-based tribals to the fullest extent possible. It is true that they are very simple and lack in the desire for greed of material possessions. Then, we find a series of incidents of insurrections and agitation at different tribal concentrated places of India, e.g., Sardah agitation of 1887 in Ranchi against the compulsory labour system and local conversions to Christianity etc. that added grist to the mill. *Paik* or *chuar* rebellion (1799), Birsha Munda revolt (1885), revolt of the Kayas of Andhra Pradesh against the exploitation and land alienation, Santal insurrection (1855), Tana Bhagat Movement among the Oraons of Ranchi (1914), Gonds and Kolams of Adilabad, Kond Maliah Movement of Orissa, are significant in this regard. When troubled, the British administration maintained a policy of *laissez faire* in respect of the tribals of country and this resulted in some concessions granted to the tribal people in the form of maintaining a *status quo ante*. Elwin said :

> ...the tribesmen had to remain at the mercy of petty officials and usurers and nothing positive by way of rehabilitation and development was achieved. The whole basis of British administration in India was to support the supporters. These vested interests were shrewed enough to benefit from every act of commission and omission of their foreign rulers. (Elwin, 10 : 1963).

In this context, S.C. Roy wrote on the administration of Justice in the tribal areas :

> The British system of law and administration has further tended to impair the solidarity of the social heads or Panchayats and the respect they formerly commanded. (From *A new deal for Tribal India*, p. 14: 1963).

It has been reflected that the tribal people were not adequately represented in the Government of India Act of 1935. We got only 24 representatives in the Provincial Legislature against a total number of members of 1,535. The British administration and the tribal communities reduced the tribal brethren to a state of penury. These people at different places groaned under the weight of their problems from time to time. A sizeable of land possessed by the tribals had gone to the hands of the non-tribals. Their rights in forest produce were trampled and very little privileges or concessions were left to them. Thus, the British administration practically evoked an unsympathetic attitude towards these groups of people, who rose in revolt sporadically in different situations, causing much more disintegration, loss of self-reliance and they were thrown into the abysmal depth of ignorance and poverty. Of course, conversion at some places opened up another vista to the already suffering and toiling tribal masses at various places of our country.

However, many political leaders, who fought against the British misrule, had inculcated in their mind the idea of tribal welfare. A.V. Thakkar and some social workers and voluntary organisations turned their attention to these problems of the tribals. Some British administrators, like Grigson, Hutton etc. unbiasedly spoke about the wretched condition of the tribal people and their speeches were reflected in various ways.

II

Independence of India and the concomitant Constitution of India spelt out many promises to these downtrodden group of people and their problems have been examined and studied from different angles in our country, which is said to be a Democratic Welfare State. Besides, it seriously appreciated the problems of the tribals and their urgency of developing them to bring them to the main fold of other stronger brethren. In the Constitution, we find various provisions for the amelioration of the conditions of the tribals, in Article 46. It runs as follows:

> The State should promote with special care the educational and economic interests of the weaker section of the people, and in particular, of the scheduled caste and scheduled tribes and shall protect them from social injustice and all forms of exploitation.

There are many other provisions to implement for the welfare of these tribals. Article 244 empowers the President to declare any area where there is concentrated a substantial number of population of the tribals as a 'Scheduled Area' under the 'Fifth Schedule' of the Constitution. Assam and N.E. India have been under the area of the 'Sixth Schedule' with different attitudes and administration with many provisions. Article 275 of the Constitution provides financial assistance, Articles 330, 332 and 334 provide reservation of seats in the Parliament and the Legislative Assemblies. Article 335 provides reservation in the services. Ministry of Welfare (T.D.), Government of India printed brochures entitled *Background Paper on Tribal Development*— in which details have been outlined and circulated for the information of the general public. Article 338 of the Constitution provides a Commissioner whose main duty will be to examine the tribal situation and to report his findings to the President through Parliament. They are to examine all matters relating to the safe guards provided in the Constitution. Of course, in pursuance of Article 46 of the Constitution, a separate department for the Scheduled Castes and Scheduled Tribes began to function from 1952. Directions have been given to create a Tribal Research Institute in each of the States, where a considerable number of Scheduled Tribes live and to have a separate Minister In-charge of the Welfare of the Scheduled Castes and Scheduled Tribes, with the Advisory Committee in the State and the District level.

In this way, many measures were taken in hand to improve the condition of the tribal people in general with the broad categories of problems, like economic, education, health and hygiene, sanitation and communication. Ever since the formulation of the First Five Year Plan, an attempt was made to improve the living condition of the tribals in general giving greater stress on their education and economic development. In the same way, the Second Five Year Plan laid more emphasis to reorganise their economy through agriculture and cottage industry, forming Co-operatives and Multipurpose Tribal Blocks, in the Third Plan period. The Fourth also laid stress on the problems identified in the earlier ones that created snags, including housing. In West Bengal, making provision for such Tribal Development Blocks was not possible due to less concentration of the tribes in a single compact area, but an alternative arrangement was made through sub-block schemes where tribals were numerically larger and constitute 50% of the total population. After this, the Central Government grant was increased and various projects were undertaken for the amelioration of the tribal people. With reference to the Fifth Plan period, in West Bengal, we find (Roy : Das : Chaudhury, 1982 : 8-9) the following:

(i) Instead of sectoral approach, a total approach was adopted for the development of the tribal areas;

(ii) To have a common policy in the National Plan, State Plans and Sub-plans;

(iii) Sub-plan areas for the tribals are to be identified and the problems of the communities are to be diagnosed and programmes chalked out with reference to each area and community;

(iv) From general section, bulk of the financial assistance is to be made and for the quantification of effort, review and adaptation of programmes by each section is to be undertaken;

(v) There should be provision for special educational assistance to the State enterprise and by the Central Government, because of its special responsibility;

(vi) The administration and the Institutional framework need be reconstituted to meet the change as well as the personal policy is to be reviewed to suit the needs of the new strategy.

As a result, we find a new institutional approach in the form of ITDP for the areas where the tribals concentration is more than 50%. Our State has altogether 33, ITDPS in the 12 districts. The latest strategy of the tribal development was through sub-plans. Here, in this new thrust, emphasis was given on the following *(Report of the Working Group on the Development of Scheduled Tribes During the 7th Five Year Plan : 1985-1990)* :

(a) tribes residing in areas of traditional tribal concentration.

(b) dispersed tribal population.

(c) primitive tribes wherever they resided, whether in the area of tribal concentration or outside.

Of course, this thrust was continued during the 6th Plan period with the emphasis (*Ibid*. p. 9) on :

(a) raising the productivity levels in production fields of tribal activities with a view to enable targetted number of families to go above the poverty line;

(b) development of human resources and upgrading education.

(c) elemination of exploitation of tribals in the field of alienation of land, money lending, debt-bondage, trade excise forest; and

(d) development of adequate infrastructures.

Besides, some more institutions were established for the welfare or the overall development of the tribal communities :

1. Integrated Tribal Development Projects (ITDP).

2. Drought Prone Area Programme (DPAP).

3. Integrated Rural Development Projects (IRDP).

4. For the Development of Backward Areas three zones were selected :

   (a) Hill Area of Darjeeling,

   (b) Sundarban Area, and

   (c) Jhargram Development.

5. There are some other organisations to look after the general development of which the principal ones are :

   (a) Comprehensive Area Development Corporation (CADC);

   (b) Small Farmer's Development Agency (SFDA); and

   (c) Command Area Development Authority (CAD).

6. (a) West Bengal Tribal Development Corporation (1975) through LAMPS to supply commodities to the tribals and to collect minor forest products and their proper sales through Government;

   (b) West Bengal Scheduled Castes and Scheduled Tribes Development and Finance Corporation (1976). The main aim for forming these Instituions are related to expedite the development and assistance to the tribals. This has been done.

...to create a delivery mechanism which would ensure optimum utilisation of all available funds for tangible and lasting benefit of the weakest of the weaker section of the community.

7. A Special Component Plan was devised to raise the standard of living through many enterprises and by avoiding usurers, brokers and money-lenders who exploit the tribals. Again, a Lodha Development Cell was constituted when the Lodhas were considered to be a Primitive Tribal Group, sometime in 1981.

III

Some measures were taken for the betterment of the tribals after Independence in various ways. Our State is a Welfare State and many such projects have been taken in hand by the Government and some voluntary organisations with finance assistance from the former. During the various plan periods thrusts were put on different matters and attempts were made accordingly to fructify them. Again, for the evaluation or rather assessment of the nature of changes some commissions were set up on an All India basis and even proliferations were made in the State level. However, recommendations were made from time to time to supplement the measures in order to scotch off constraints, if there be any, in the work. It is true that rehabilitation is regarded as a very important phase of development of the weaker sections. As such, a good number of rehabilitation colonies were started initially with the Cental Government money and State Government also had initiated it with their resources. It is true that rehabilitation is a more abiding and scientific procedure: it requires more scrutiny before implementation of the scheme for the intended purpose. But so far, it has been observed that most of the rehabilitation colonies set up by the tribals were not properly scrutinised before the plan was drafted. It was implemented either by the voluntary organisation or on behalf of the Government or by the district administration directly.

In the case of Lodhas, initially some measures were taken by the Home (Police) Department as the Lodhas were considered to be a 'Criminal Tribe' till the revocation of the C.T. Act in 1952. Kukai village, under the Police Station of Keshiary, one such attempt was made under the guidance of a social worker named P.C. Midya, who took keen interest and, as such, a Co-operative was formed and some land as well as agricultural implements and bullocks were purchased to make the Lodhas a 'settled people', and to develop among them a spirit of the 'sense of belonging'. Rehabilitation of these people not only includes the housing facilities, but also other subsidiaries, such as, purchase of bullocks, goats, other implements and seeds along with the purchase of land and reclamation of them. This indicates that most of the rehabilitation schemes implemented so far were agriculture based, whether the people intended to be rehabilitated in an area of good agricultural facilities or were basically agriculture minded or not. The main object of rehabilitation is to provide the beneficiaries a stable economic background, so that by getting such benefits, they might equate themselves with other more progressive communities of the country, gradually binding up the economic and social distances so long prevailing amongst them.

During the Second and the Third Five Year Plans, all these attempts were made by our State Government in many places. Bharat Mahajati Mondali (1951) was chosen to undertake the welfare work with Governmental assistance directly. The Totos at Totopara were initially given priority along with a tribal welfare centre by the Government directly. Initially, Bharat Mahajati Mondali (1951) and the Lutheran World Service undertook the work of welfare of these communities and, as a result, we find Schools - Primary and High upto Class VIII standard - and an Ashram Hostel, a set of staff quarters were constructed to help educate this isolated group of Toto boys. Here, a weaving centre was also started. The Nepalese from the border areas gradually infiltrated when the 'reserve' order was withdrawn. Of course, the Totos have economic symbiosis with the Nepalese who provided them some sort of employment opportunities during production of orange, as labourers. This resulted ultimately in the encroachment of the land of the Totos and now very shrewdly they are being exploited, though Government arranged for irrigation and the plantation of trees, specially areca-cuts, are there by the Totos. They are also given the facilities of land reclamation since 1952. Lutheran World Service also provided a Medical Centre for the welfare of the Totos in isolation, and a subsidiary Health Centre is in the process of making.

There are a small rural library, a community hall, a Welfare Centre, a new Guest House and a Staff Quarters Complex which normally draw attention of any casual visitor to this place. Attempts were also made to develop the habit of cleanliness and to make them use the preventive and curative drugs for their immediate relief against the unseen diseases. They also attempted to improve the agricultural methods and techniques, and tries their best to overcome the problems of land alienation and other forms of exploitation.

However, the present trend of welfare activities after the inclusion of the Totos as Primitive Tribal Group has been discussed in different chapters in respect of economy, education, health and sanitation.

The Birhors, a small tribal group, have a concentration in Purulia district. For their development a rehabilitation colony was initiated and the colony was named as *Bhupati Palli* colony, after the name of the then Minister of Tribal Welfare. As usual, all the rehabilitation facilities were extended to them and ultimately it was found that nothing tangible had come of it. Fundamentally, they are a gathering-hunting tribe who exploited the nature, but they should have been passed through many socialisation processes under the careful supervision of one social worker. As these are all through Government managements, they suffered from initiative and many other difficulties. As a result, the project is almost a failure.

Of the Birhors at Bhupati Palli Rehabilitation Colony, out of 16 families 10 have left to their original settlement. The hostel is not functioning and the school is not running properly. The projects and the families extended to them are being discussed separately, itemwise, along with the budget provision.

After the rehabilitation schemes being implemented for the tribal groups, a few such rehabilitation colonies for the Lodhas were initiated by some voluntary organisations. One such colony was initiated at Auligeria in the Police Station of Jhargram (Midnapur) under the stewardship of Late Prof. Priyaranjan Sen, who was the Secretary of the Harijan Sevak Sangh, Bengal Branch. They were to have rehabilitated 45 families within an allocation of Rs. 1,500/- per family. Facilities were extended to all the families to own a cottage industry, purchase land, bullocks etc. Of course, due to the patronage of the then Congress Government, Prof. Sen started a Pre-Basic School, Basic (Primary) School etc. From different sources, he procured money to construct a Link Road (non-metalled) from the metalled road (Garh Salboni) of the jungle covered side and ultimately touched the village Auligeria, newly named at that time as Santigarh or 'the place of peace'. This village was a seat of the criminals.

Secondly, a full-fledged colony was started at Dholkat-Pukuria under the direct supervision of Bharat Sevashram Sangh, Calcutta. Previously this forest-covered village was selected by the *Swamijis* (monks) to be used as a place for resting. But when the Government, i.e., the Tribal Welfare Department approached to take initiative in a constructive work of rehabilitation, the monks readily agreed to part with it. In the same manner, land purchase, construction of huts, purchase of agricultural implements, seeds etc. were arranged as parts of the programme of Welfare work. Thus, so far it was working well, as per direction of the

Tribal Welfare Department and the items which were in existence there were also properly utilised. In course of time, one Ashram Hostel for the Lodha boys was started (1966) and later a Primary School upgraded differently upto Class VIII standard, as a Junior High School. Apparently, it looked as though the scheme was a complete success, but no fundamental change in the life-style of the Lodhas could be effected by this. During 1964, in the Lodha-Santal riots two Lodhas of the two Rehabilitation Centres were victimised by some infuriated groups of the other communities, e.g. the Santals and the Mahatos-due to their persistent involvement in criminal activities.

In the third phase of rehabilitation, a place was selected at Daharpur - a multi-tribal and caste village. Initially 31 families, and later 20, were settled there. The responsibility of the work was given to a voluntary organisation called Samaj Sevak Sangh, in which some Social Scientists were associated. Considering the political pressure and other difficulties, the said organisation constituted a rehabilitation sub-committee in which they included three Government officials, viz., the B.D.O. of the area, Special Officer, S.C. and S.T. Department of the District Headquarters and one Assistant Director for the State level. This facilitated the change in programme or items which were considered to be expensive and repetitive. More money was spent for the purchase of land, almost all the huts were repaired and about eight huts were newly constructed for those who had no shelter at all; one community-hut or dormitory for the bachelors and a social worker-cum-guest house were also constructed allowing the facilities of weaving, tailoring etc. along with a small library house. Subsequently, one Junior Basic School was started and the first Ashram Hostel for the Junior Lodha boys (infant Class to Class V standard) was also started sometime in 1964, after the All India Conference of the De-notified Tribes held in Delhi at the Old Parliament House in which Late Lal

Bahadur Sastri was the President and in which the then Prime Minister Jawaharlal Nehru and U.N. Dhebar attended. A sizeable number of anthropologists were also present at the meeting from various parts of the country to discuss the ameliorative measures for these backward classes. As per decision, the State Governments were directed to implement the Schemes discussed and resolved in the conference.

Again, at Bhumij Dhansol (under Binpur P.S. of Jhargram Subdivision) another rehabilitation colony was set up. This was a measure taken to rehabilitate the Lodhas, who were then having rough weather due to a communal riot between the Lodhas in one hand and the Santals and the Mahatos on the other. The entire village was set fire due to constant act of thieving and dacoity which peeved the Santals so much so that they took a unanimous decision in destroying the Lodha hutments with an attempt to assault them. Ultimately, the rehabilitation colony was very much attractive materially and the Lodha boys were sent to Daharpur Ashram Hostel and for that purpose seats of the Ashram were increased by about 10 seats for the Lodha boys in totalling 30.

Again, sometime in 1974, a village named Chhoto Jhauri, under the Police Station of Gopiballavpur, a border of Orissa (only 1.5 km.) more than 22 Lodhas (almost all male persons) were arrested due to dacoity in some villages. The then Inspector General of Police, West Bengal, took initiative to rehabilitate them through the Institute of Social Research and Applied Anthropology, of which he is the President, wells were dug, social worker and a constable well versed in agriculture and kindergarden were put at the centre and ultimately a good relationship developed among the local people through socialisation and education. Ever even today no crime has been recorded and no participation of the Lodhas during Patina (Nayagram P.S.)

mass killing which took place sometime in 1979 (Table 3.8).

This then was the nature of rehabilitation programme of the Lodhas - the so-called Primitive Tribe. Of course, during that period some provisions were made to accommodate the Lodha children through Ashram Hostels at different Lodha concentrated areas. Later on, the Government through district officials took initiative to be involved in the rehabilitation work by constructing cottages, developing roads, digging wells, constructing school buildings, giving goats and birds, agricultural implements etc, here and there, wherever possible. But ultimately most of them ended in a fiasco failed or flopped.

For the Kharia tribe, the Government took an initiative. It has been mentioned that similar rehabilitation colonies for the Santals and even for some Scheduled Caste people also were approved for the betterment of the suffering people. However, at Bansgarh in Binpur P.S., under Jhargram Subdivision, 30 Kharia families were rehabilitated, but the ultimate fate of the Kharias was to abandon the colony as the management was in the hands of the Government. Another such attempt was made at Mukutmonipur in the district of Bankura. It housed 30 families. The Kharia colony at Bansgarh (Midnapur) was an utter failure—only a few families were there under difficult situation. Out of the 30 families of the Kharias at Mukutmonipur (Bankura) 15 continued to live and others left the colony.

IV

Thus, it is clear from the above discussion that colonies under the direct supervision of the Government faced terrible difficulties, which prompted the decampment of the inmates, whereas in other places the voluntary organisations took more initiative to look after the problems as well as to their remedial measures and got good goings for the colonies. Apparently, this suggests that the Government management, in respect of rehabilitation has been an abortive attempt so far, and in all these schemes there were good many short-comings and loop-holes in their functioning. No provision for solution of the psycho-emotional problems was made, but in the case of the voluntary organisation, they adjusted all these through their own resources. Deviation from the programmes, when found essential, were effected by the sponsors on their own responsibility and they had to justify the causes there to the Director, Tribal Welfare Department, Government of West Bengal. In this connection, it may be mentioned that progress in all the rehabilitation colonies under different organisations are not the same. Those who followed all Government directions had to face more problems and they did not feel the actual need of the people too only they respected the Government directives. Besides, in most of the cases, no provision for the integration or mixing with other people of different categories were arranged, except by the Samaj Sevak Sangh in which both the Social Scientists, Social Workers, administrators and the target groups had the opportunity of discussing the problems across the table. Here, ambitious ideas of the planners were flourished which are generally utopian in nature, but have no relationship with the down-to-earth reality. In the hostels themselves there was a provision to keep non-Lodha tribal students who along with their studies can work as sentinels or served as guards against the inherent misdeeds of the Lodha children. Naturally, tension was rare. These were some activities or the measures taken by the Government before these tribals were included as P.T.G. In most cases, the sponsors or the administration observed this more in the breach and failed to articulate the affiliated community in the broader psycho-social areas impressing upon others who need amity. Naturally, trouble shoot up which further aggravate the wretched condition of the Lodhas who bear the inseparable stigma of criminality with them.

Due to change of Government, a new political climate started blowing and in the Panchayat-based Society, many things have been, and are being, done through the Sabhadhipati (President of the Zilla Parishad) and the Advisory Committee meant for the tribals. In spite of their democratisation, the progress is to be assessed, while evaluation is made. Constant killings of the Lodhas (Table: 3.8) during this time has actually blotted the Indian Democracy and the remedial measures are more expensive and fruitless.

Part Two
OBSERVATIONS

5

Economic Development

I

It has been reiterated that the tribal groups, in general, and the Primitive Tribal Groups, in particular, have long association with poverty and hunger and, as such, they with their crude technology utilise the ecological and environmental resources in their circumstantial exigencies, but these are not sufficient enough to reflect a state of sound economy. Naturally, welfare or development schemes meant for these tribal groups through constitutional support requires full analysis of the cultural background to find out the various forced operating in them. It is true that in many cases the result of development might be confined to a smaller section of the group due to uneven percolation of development efforts. In this context, Dube (1988 : 46) says :

> Economic development is need oriented, endogamous, self-reliant, ecologically sound and based on structural transformation. It is aimed at those who have been deprived and exploited. It recognises the importance of equality, freedom of expression, convivality and creativity. No universal model is to be imposed.

We have to consider carefully the various projects and schemes sanctioned by the respective District Advisory Committees or other appropriate committees who are being entrusted to design and to implement these for the Primitive Tribal Groups in West Bengal where these people have genuinely different cultural and sometimes ecological background. We all know that the development programmes are time-bound to achieve the desired future, considering the felt-needs of the people, and to equate them with the proportionately stronger brethren of the society. We can easily visualise the condition of the people as they are close to hunger and poverty. Their impoverished condition leaves them with the imprint of less productivity and ill-health. Insignificant literacy among them fail them to understand the situation in proper perspective in and around, and it becomes a continuous pull force towards backwardness, that already prevails, and create disillusionment about others as also narrow down their world view. This also leads to a position of inescapable maladjustment by occasionally surfacing many violent incidents. In this connection, it can be said that the District Advisory Committees generally provide some items of welfare for these groups of people, considering their burning problems. Sometimes the old formula of stereotyped welfare schemes which have no practical base to bring about any stable change in the economic structure in the group behavour are being suggested for them. Table 5.1 reflects the number of projects initiated for the people for 1980-81 and 1989-90:

Table 5.1
Number of Projects/Schemes Undertaken

Sl. No.	*Project Sanctioned since 1981-1989*	*Toto*	*Birhor*	*Lodha*	*Kheria*
1.	Community-Agriculture	+	-	-	-
2.	Soil Conservation	+	-	+	+
3.	Irrigation	+	+	+	+
4.	5 H.P. Pumpset	-	-	+	-
5.	Agricultural implements	-	+	+	+
6.	Excavation of Tank	-	+	+	+
7.	Minikit	-	-	+	+
8.	Supply of Bullock	-	-	+	+
9.	Dairy or Milch Cow Scheme	+	+	+	+
10.	Piggery	+	-	-	-
11.	Sheep	-	-	-	+
12.	Goatery	-	+	+	+
13.	Poultry	+	+	-	-
14.	Fruit Bearing Plants	+	-	+	+
15.	Babulgrass	-	-	+	+
16.	Rope Making	-	+	-	-
17.	Preparation of Leaf Plates	-	+	-	-
18.	Cultivation of Mat Stick and Mat Making	-	-	+	+
19.	Trolley	-	-	+	-
20.	Club-House	-	-	+	-

+ = Allotted. - = Not Allotted.

In order to summarise the projects, considering the needs of the group of people, a separate table has been prepared from the above table (Table 5.1) and numbered as Table 5.2. In this table the items of the projects have been shown tribe-wise :-

Table 5.2
Projects/Schemes Sanctioned Tribe-wise

Sl. No.	*Name of the Tribe*	*Projects Sanctioned*
1.	Toto	All projects sanctioned out of 20 except 4, 5, 6, 7, 8, 11, 12, 15, 16, 17, 18, 19, 20.
2.	Birhor	All projects sanctioned out of 20 except 1, 2, 4, 7, 8, 10, 11, 14, 15, 18, 19, 20.
3.	Lodha	All projects sanctioned out of 20 except 1, 10, 11, 13, 16, 17.
4.	Kharia/Kheria	All projects sanctioned out of 20 except 1, 4, 10, 13, 16, 17, 18, 19, 20.

While examining the contents of the project items, it appears that in almost all the cases greater emphasis has been laid on to these people for the development of agriculture which, according to the planners, can sustain the people and can give them more time to be engaged for the purpose of generating gainful employment within it. But, in actuality, the utopain outlook never stood to scrutiny and the framers of the projects/schemes are making repeated mistakes without considering the final upshot or the outcome. It may be noted here that a community agricultural scheme was suggested only of the Totos as the group of people live in a small territory. But in the case of others, some families have been extended to sometimes through soil conservation, sometimes through providing irrigational facilities, sometimes by supplying agricultural implements, pump-sets, bullocks, minikits etc. Next to these we find instances of encouragement to maintain domestic animals, like milch cows, goats, sheep, pigs and poultry birds, occasionally with an ambitious idea of raising a dairy farm. Remarkable breakthrough has been made and sanctioning grants for pisciculture by excavating moribund tanks. Again, fruit-bearing trees along with social forestry scheme have been supplied to some of these groups, like the Lodhas, with a view to keep them supplied in tree-planting and starting small-scale industries, specially in the laterite regions. *'Babui'* or *'Sabai'* grass plantations have been encouraged among these people with which they can make ropes by twisting its leaves. These activities are confined to the Lodha and the Kheria only. There are a few cases where the Lodhas have been extended the advantage of mat-making by cultivating the mat-stick plants. Leaf-plate making out of the available jungle leaves has been extended to the Birhors. Work for road construction at some places, trolley and rickshaw pulling, establishing shops and stalls and constructing huts by the Lodha labourers are being done along with all other tribes through Governemt efforts. One temple has been constructed for the Totos and a club house has been sanctioned for the Lodhas by the Government. These are the continuous schemes and projects which have been sanctioned for these groups of people by the appropriate authorities with an idea to improve their economic condition which, in turn, will bring other changes for the overall betterment of these tribes.

II

While verifying the schemes and examining the nature of benefits accruing out of these schemes, it appears that 15 Lodha villages at different places, 4 Kheria villages and the entire Toto community, as also Birhors, have been studied by the researcher.

Table 5.3

Particulars of Sample Villages (Surveyed)

Sl. No.	*Tribe with Family*	*Name of Village*	*District*	*Total No. of Family*
1.	Toto (163)	Totopara	Jalpaiguri (163)	163
2.	Birhor (47)	Bhupati-Palli, Baridi, Bararia	Purulia (47)	47
3.	Lodha (288)	Daharpur, Kasba, Birkar, Jatirampur, Kulidanbatitaki, Gonua, Krishna-rakshitchak, Nakrakhudi, Radhanagar, Arasini, Satsole, Dhole-kat, Chandabila, Manibpur, Bhururchati,	Midnapur (288)	288
4.	Kharia (216)	Pataghar, Shankhabhanga, Chakadoba, Lagadari, Rajkusma, Ashakathi, Jhatiara.	Midnapur (115)	115
		Maguria, Damodarpur	Purulia (41)	41
		Katiyam, Mukutmonipur, Jolhori	Bankura (60)	60

Besides, many more villages have already been visited casually by the scribe while conducting the survey. Item-wise verification shows that :-

I. Community agricultural scheme meant for the Totos of Jalpaiguri and for this purpose a sum of Rs. 1,73,440 has been sanctioned during 1986-87, but the entire amount is yet to be spent, i.e. Rs.1,65,803 only has been spent.

II. *Soil Conversion* : For all the tribes, except the Birhors the scheme for soil conservation has been sanctioned. During the year 1988-89, a scheme for this purpose amounting to a sum of Rs. 1,50,000 was sanctioned for the Totos. During the survey the scheme was expected to start, but no effective step was taken in that direction. Naturally, further verification will have to be appended. Again, a sum of Rs. 6,83,436 has been allotted for the purpose of soil conservation in the Lodha villages in the district of Midnapur. Out of the 15 villages selected at random, 7 have the advantage of getting such benefits. 62 families were earmarked to get the benefits but, in reality, 52 persons got little money (most of the beneficiaries have forgotten) to prepare their land for making it agriculturally suitable only for one year. Rumours go that money meant for this purpose has been spent on heads other than soil conservation, which could have facilitated agricultural productions. Some of the informants again alleged that in order to improve the land it requires more money which should be allotted to them, at least for three consecutive years. Since 1982-83 to 1986-87, an amount of Rs. 26,723 had been granted for Kharia village. Officially, it was meant to subsidise 90 families but, in fact, 78 families were given the facilities. Though they were supposed to have prepared the field by raising the contour ridges so as to hold water during the rainy season for agricultural purposes, it was not done. But in village Sankhabhanga under Binpur Police Station of Midnapur, no trace of it is visible now though it has been mentioned in the records.

III. Irrigational facilities have been extended to all the communities in these districts and for this purpose a sum of Rs. 7,26,518 has been allotted. Table 5.4 shows details of money sanctioned for the purpose to different places.

Table 5.4
Irrigation Schemes

Community		*Scheme*	*Year*	*Amount Sanctioned (Rs.)*	*Target*	*Present Condition*
TOTO (Sanctioned Rupees 4,17,500)	1.	Pujagaon Irrigation Scheme.	1985-86	25,000	1 (for 12 families).	Not functioning.
	2.	,,	1985-86	25,000	1(for 10 families).	,,
	3.	,,	1987-88	50,000	1 (for 30 families).	,,
	4.	Protection of Pujagaon Irrigation-Scheme.	1988-89	17,500	1(for 30 families).	Functioning.
	5.	Banjokhola Irrigation Scheme.	1985-86	25,000	1	,,
	6.	Irrigation Scheme near New Inspection Bungalow.	1985-86	25,000	1 (for 14 families).	Functioning
	7.	Irrigation Scheme at Totopara.	1986-87	1,00,000	1	Failure

	8.	Irrigation Scheme of Daljho.	1987-88	50,000	1 (for 20 families).	Functioning.
	9.	Extension of Irrigation Scheme Bonjokhola.		50,000	1 (for 18 families).	,,
	10.	Excavation of Irrigational Canal.	1987-88	50,000	1 (for 30 families).	Failure
	Total				**4,17,500**	
BIRHOR (Sanctioned Rupees 60,000)	1.	Dug well for Irrigation	1983-84	48,000	6	3-functioning, 3-Failure
	2.	Reservoir for Irrigation	,,	12,000	1	Functioning.
	Total			**60,000**		
LODHA (Sanctioned Rupees. 23,47,416).	1.	R.C.C. Ring well for irrigation drinking purposes.	1981-82	Not found from office	1	Out of order.
			1983-84	4,406 (approx.)	3	1-Functioning, 2-Out of order.
			1984-85	Not Found	1	Not completed.
			1985-86	11,200	4	2-Out of order. 2-Functioning.

		1986-87	10,780	2	1-Out of order. 1-Functioning.
		1988-89	1,500 (approx.)	1	Functioning.
	2. Sinking of Shallow Tubewell	1981-82	28,000	3	2-Out of order. 1-Absent.
		1983-84	96,153	29	7-Functioning.
	Total	**Rs. 152,039**			
KHARIA not available)	1. R.C.C. Ring well	1984-85	16,000	2	Nil
		1985-86	10,000	1	Nil
	2. Kutcha Dug well	1983-84	9,772	5	5
		1984-85	61,207	5	3
		1985-86	-	26	7 1-Incomplete.
	Total	**Rs. 96,779**			

In Totopara, an ambitious plan was chalked out extending irrigational facilities and this was to have covered the entire village. River water was to be stored for being used in agriculture. Actually, 4 minor schemes are found to be operating and the others are yet to be completed. Again, about 6 such minor projects proved to be failures. The statements reveal that six dug-wells and one tank have been excavated in the villages inhabited by the Birhors, but while verifying only 4 are found to be operative. In 15 Lodha villages, 15 R.C.C. ring-wells and kutcha wells were sanctioned during the year 1981-82 and upto 1988-89. Along with this, irrigation through shallow wells were sanctioned for the Lodhas. The total number of shallow wells, numbering 32, were allotted but on field verification it was recorded the 5 R.C.C./kutcha wells and 7 shallow tube-wells are in existence in the village, like Satsol, Chandabila and Jotirampur. For the Kharias, R.C.C. ring wells and kutcha wells were allotted, the details of which are recorded on Table 5.5.

Table 5.5
Details of R.C.C. Ring Wells and Kutcha Wells for the Kharias in Midnapur District

Schemes	*Block*	*Village*	*Year*	*Target*	*Amount*	*Present condition*
R.C.C. Ring well	Binpur -II	Pataghar	1984-85	1	8,000	Absent (Nil)
"	"	Sankha-bhanga	1985-86	1	10,000	"
"	"	Lagadari	1984-85	1	8,000	"
Kutcha Dug well	Binpur -II	Patagarh	1984-85	5	6,120	3
			1985-86	4	6,896	4
			1983-84	5	6,120	5
"	"	Ashakanthi and Rajkusuma	1985-86	3	3,672	1
"	"	Lagadari	1985-86	10	12,240	8
"	"	Sankha-bhanga	1985-86	5	8,500	1 (incomplete)
"	"	Jhatiara	1985-86	4	6,800	4
			Total		**Rs. 76,348**	

IV. Pump sets to facilitate better irrigational system were sanctioned only for the Lodhas where they have exhibited their aptitude for cultivation. Though 7 sets were sanctioned, while surveying, only 4 sets could be found to function.

V. Agricultural implements were distributed to the Birhors, Lodhas and the Kharias. These implements consist of spade, digging sticks, sickle and other ancillary implements. For this purpose, a sum of Rs. 27,185 (only in the villages) has been sanctioned. But some informants told the scribe that all those are not in existence now, as there is no evidence of supply of those articles to the recipients at all. Some people have their own traditional implements and they try to equip themselves when needed with great difficulty.

Table 5.6

Distribution of Agricultural Implements to the Beneficiaries

Name of Tribe	*Year Sanctioned*	*Amount, Beneficiaries*	*Target*	*Actual*
Birhor	1983-84	10,000	47	3
Lodha	1981-82	1,925		
	1984-85	1,900	32	23
	1985-86	4,075		Not at all
	1986-87	3,910		
Kharia	1982-83	5,000	10	Nil
	Total	**Rs. 27,185**		

In this connection, a tale can be retold. Sometime in 1984, Mr. A.K. Deb, IAS was the District Magistrate and Collector of Midnapur. He was very sympathetic towards the tribals and he decided to distribute a few household and agricultural implements free of cost to the Lodhas before the Puja holiday's amounting

Rs. 100 per head per family. When the scribe came to know of this scheme, he informed the Collector that the Lodhas, after receiving those articles, would sell them out on their way back home from the Block Office of Belda. Mr. Deb was requested to verify the truth of the statement. Accordingly, he came and stayed at Bidisa for the entire period of distribution in plain clothes. The author was also waiting for the return of the Lodhas by that route. Almost all the Lodhas thus benefited were asked by Mr. Deb. They candidly replied that after selling all those articles in the nearby market, they got cash money of Rs. 45/- to Rs. 48/- each. The implements consisted of a bucket, a string, a spade, a sickle, a scythe, a hurricane lantern etc. for each person. They parted with them all and in lieu thereof purchased eatables and some other things from the local market where they disembarked from the bus, and come back merrily.

VI. Excavation of tank is meant for pisciculture and this was extended to the Birhors, the Lodhas and the Kharias. This scheme was taken up to encourage the people for supplementing their economy by means of pisciculture. But in almost all the places where an individual is the beneficiary, it is a complete failure. Table 5.6 indicates the situation.

Table 5.6

Details of Excavation of Tank for the Lodhas (Surveyed Villages) in Midnapur

Sl. No.	*Name of the Villages*	*Year*	*Total amount Sanctioned*	*Target*	*Present condition*
1.	Gonua	81-82	20,000	1	Not excavated
2.	Daharpur	83-84	30,000	2	,,

3. Daharpur	85-86	3,000	1	Not excavated
4. Kulidan-batitaki	83-84	4,500	3	1-excavated
5. Jatirampur	83-84	12,000	8	3-excavated
6. Jatirampur	85-86	6,000	2	
7. Birkar	Date is not available		3	1-excavated
8. Kasba	83-84	1,500	1	1-excavated
9. Krishnarak-shitchalk	88-89	4,000	1	1-under cons-truction
10. Nakrakhudi	88-89	4,000	1	Not executed
11. Bhururchati	86-87	1,500	1	1-under cons-truction
12. Bhururchati	86-87	4,000	1	1-under cons-truction
13. Manibpur	83-84	3,000	2	2-not in order
14. Arasihi	83-84	3,000	2	2-not in order
15. Radhanagar	83-84	4,500	3	1-excavated
16. Satsole	83-84	1,500	1	1-not in order
17. Satsole	86-87	4,000	1	1-excavated
18. Chandabila	85-86	14,600 (apporx)	1	1-excavated

VII. Some provisions have already been made for distribution of minikit in order to facilitate agricultural operations, especially during the paddy cultivation season. Table 5.7 indicates distribution of the minikits in the villages inhabited by the Lodhas and the Kharias showing the number of target families and the actual beneficiaries.

Table 5.7
Distribution of Mini-kits to Target Families and the Beneficiaries

Community	*Year*	*Amount sanctioned*	*Target*	*Actual beneficiaries*
Lodha	1982-83	Rs. 1,550	18	14
Kheria	1982-83	Rs. 37,000	37	3

VIII. For supplying bullocks in connection with agriculture the Government spent lots of money. It is wonder of wonders that no bullock is to be found now, except in a few particular families, where these were purchased in recent months, i.e. before the field study was undertaken. This is a chronic malady in the matter of extending welfare measures by alloting bullocks. From the experience, it is suggested that the authorities should stop this sham show of things. However, it requires an aptitude to maintain the bullocks to get work out of them. During the lean months, it is difficult for the Lodhas to maintain the bullocks, and it requires a watchful care and sustaining efforts to do so. In almost all the cases, the bullocks were sold out as soon as these were received. At the time of the survey, many of them informed that old and infirm bullocks were supplied to them by the Government officials and those died a natural death only after a few days. With the experience gained out of this, the planners could have paused and pondered and stopped repeating the mistake without asking the beneficiaries as to why they were doing such things. No alternative was either sought or suggested to them.

IX. *Dairy or milch-cow supply scheme :* This scheme is only operative among the Lodhas and the Kharias. From the very beginning, even in earlièr times, this scheme had a sad and tragic tale to tell. Even before the Lodhas were recognised as P.T.G., one such ambitious scheme was handled by a Lodha graduate who is now engaged in the I.T.D.P. office, in his own village of Chaksahapur under Debra P.S. It ended in a fiasco. In spite of past experience, the scheme is still in vogue and tons of money has been spent for this purpose. However, the number of target families was about 51, but only 20 families of the sample villages admitted that they received the milch-cow, none of them being in a position to show their existence, e.g., the villages of Dholkat, Chandabila, Manibpur and Arasini. In case of the Kharias, two families of village Katiyan Block Ranibandh, Dist. Bankura had received the milch-cows, of which one has been sold and the other is found to be in a poor shape. These are all meant for individual families. Again, it can be said in this connection that the Totos and the Birhors were given a scheme of dairy development. For the Toto, Rs. 31,015 had been allotted during the year 1986-87, and a sum of Rs. 37,400 in Bhupati Palli, Rs. 10,000 for Bararia and Rs. 10,650 on Barida in the district of Purulia for the Birhors. Except for Bhupati Palli (where a few have survived) none are in existence in case of the Birhors. The small dairy at Bhupati Palli of Purulia district is looked after by 6 Birhor families and the condition of those surviving is not very encouraging. But among the Totos, it is a bit hopeful story, the animals are more or less in a better condition.

Poultry birds were given to the Totos and the Birhors. For this purpose, a sum of Rs. 28,925 (for 1986-87 and 1987-88) was spent for each Toto and the Birhor families. Of this, Rs. 1,800 has been spent for Bhupati Palli.

X. The piggery scheme is being operated in Totopara where about all the families were given the facilities and, for this purpose, a sum of Rs. 29,000 and Rs. 28,506 have been allotted and the scheme is on the rails.

XI. The Kharias were allotted a few sheep in the shape of a project, but none is in existence now.

Table 5.8
Sheep for the Kharias

Block - Binpur II	*Amount - Rs. 6,000/-*
Village-Year 1985-86	
Ashakanthi & Rajkusma	Present condition
Target family - 2	Nothing is in existence now
Beneficiaries - 2	

XII. A goatary scheme was subsequently included as a family oriented scheme. This was suggested and allotted to the Lodhas from the very beginning. Almost all the tribes, except the Totos, were extended to this project. Though the officers were very careful about the genuineness of the sale of the goats, practically they have had no control over the system. Once one B.D.O. very politely reported on the score as follows :

> Please don't ask me about the procedure. I along with my Veterinary Officer generally go to the spot where the transaction is made. The Veterinary Officer is to check and certify the condition of the goats. Then money is given to seller in our presence and the market owner is to give a signed receipt. Then what happens we are not allowed to see.

However, in our sample survey, villages during 1981-82, 1986-87 and 1988-89, goats were supplied to the Lodhas. The target number of families, as per statement of the B.D.Os, was 87 in the 9 Lodha villages, but actual survey reveals that only 45 persons were extended these facilities.

Of course, according to some informants, the number of goats vary between two and eight. Very recently, due to introduction of family oriented scheme, it has become almost compulsory for all the families to keep goats. But in actuality, even 20% of the total number cannot be found to exist.

The situation in the case of the Kharias is almost similar. During the year 1982-83, a sum of Rs. 32,239 was sanctioned for the two villages of Pataghar and Shimulpal. They could have got about 200 goats. Actually, as the Kharias told, they were given 140-144 goats some died or sold.

XIII. *Poultry* : Poultry birds were supplied to the Totos and the Birhors. Again, every year from 1983-84, a sum of Rs. 4,360 was sanctioned for the Birhors. In addition, during 1986-87 and 1987-88, a sum of Rs. 28,925 was allotted to the Totos and the Birhors for this purpose. During the survey, however, it was found that nothing was in existence.

XIV. *Fruit-bearing plants and social forestry* : This is another costly experiment done for the Primitive Tribal Groups since the inception of the welfare projects. This scheme was extended to all the PTG's, except the Birhors. The scheme is particularly successful among the Totos where bountiful nature encouraged them to embark upon such an endeavour in their blissful surroundings. Trees, specially arecanuts, were given to them and those are yielding bumper fruits to the Totos. According to the informants, such a project was undertaken long ago, and in 1983-84 and 1988-89 the trees planted survived, to an extent of 50%.

Similarly, the plantation of fruit-bearing trees was done among the Lodhas and the Kharias also. The plants included mango, guava, jack-fruit, lemon, lichis etc. It is interesting to note that during a decade, a sum of Rs. 3,60,640 and Rs. 1,12,885 (approximately) only has been spent for the Lodhas and the Kharias. Survey in the sample villages revealed that actually the plants were given to them without any demonstration and these plants almost wilted at the time of distribution. Naturally, the project is a grand failure. No attempt has been made to search out any alternative scheme.

XV. *Babui* or *Sabai grass cultivation and rope-making*: This is another economic incentive extended to the Lodhas and the Kharias. Here, a grass-like plant is generally sown in the arid land before the advent of rains and these begin to grow. Finally, when these grow to a certain height, they are harvested from the field and dried up. With the help of an ordinary wooden machine these are twisted and made into ropes for use. Some Lodhas of Keshiary Police Station, specially of village Satsol, are engaged in this work. This scheme is functioning well among the Kharias. In the Kharia villages, like Patagarh, Ashakanthi, Rajkusma, Lagadari, Jatiara and Chakdoba, the actual beneficiaries are 28 of the 35 target families. However, the Kharias show a bit of success in this regard. From this rope, house construction, *Charpoi* building or cot thatching are made and these are sold in the local market from which they get a little earning. It is reported that these plants grow quickly and sometimes twice in the year these can be harvested for use.

XVI. Another rope-making project was initiated among the Birhors. The Birhors are traditionally adept in preparing ropes out of the bark of trees (*Chop*) and these have a good market in the locality. The Birhors are allowed to collect barks through their traditional way from the nearby jungles, and for twisting, a machine has been provided to them. But the Birhors are not capable to use the machine, as they have no training and no such facilities have been extended to them Rs. 10,000 (approx.) has been sanctioned for this purpose.

XVII. Another interesting way of encouragement without training has been extended to the Birhors, viz. preparation of leaf-plate. A machine has been purchased but nobody has yet been trained up. For this purpose, a sum of Rs. 28,000 has, it is shown, been spent. The implement, it is reported, has been lying idle.

XVIII. *Cultivation of mat-sticks and weaving of mats* : This has been given only to the Lodhas. Mat-making in the Police Stations of Sabong and Debra is done on a commercial scale. Even the caste Hindu people have availed of this opportunity and they are augmenting their income to some extent by this. But in this matter, what is very much necessary is a systematic training of the workers. This is not being done, because the Lodhas are an indolent lot - not industrious and painstaking by habit.

XIX. Besides, some Lodhas have been encouraged to own a few trolleys they use for carrying luggages and other merchandise on hire. In the same way, one or two Lodhas have been extended help to set up stalls for selling nick-knacks. It is very difficult to assess how far these individuals will stick to this trade. In the name of a 'Family Benefit Scheme', a mixed project - as per needs of the families - has been implemented for the Birhors and the Lodhas. This includes supply of milch-cows and encouraging cultivation of mat-sticks, as also mat-making. This project has been extended to some of the Lodhas also. Such family-oriented schemes have been launched during the year 1988-89. We are yet to see its results. Here, reportedly a sum ranging upto Rs. 2,000 per family has been allotted for various developmental activities with a view to helping the members of the family who will be in a position to earn something out of these projects.

Bullocks, milch-cows, goats etc. are considered to be important items of investment which have been proved to be a case of grand failure.

With regard to industrial encouragement, the Tribal Advisory Committee initiated a new ambitious step to encourage the Lodhas through 'Printex Works' for printing of cloth, like bed-sheets, window screens etc. As a matter of fact, a sum of Rs. 1,93,835, vide 129(18) ITDP, JHR dated 13.3.1984 has been shown disbursed on this score. Subsequently, the Eighth Five Year Plan of Midnapur district (for 1990-95) corroborated the same, (page : IV-349) under the heading of 'Assets created' (since 1981 upto 1989) for development of the Lodha community in item 22 - 'Printex'. It shows that 90 families have been benefited (copy enclosed). Attempts have also been made to find out the Lodha families involved in this, as well as to verify the fact through the proprietor of the 'Printex Works'. His statement is in the negative (copy of letter annexed). But the same type of printing of cloth by a voluntary organisation at Dalkati Lodha village proved a success.

However, as an alternative to agriculture and other jobs, it is always a welcome move. Besides, some roads have been repaired or constructed and a good number of huts have been constructed during the period under survey as the Government report goes.

III

It is an accepted truth that all sorts of developmental projects/schemes undertaken for the Primitive Tribal Groups are meant to elevate their economic base by opening up self-employment facilities for gainful purposes, to satisfy their basic needs and on the basis of which quality of their life-style can be improved. This is expected to surmount the economic inequality which is still haunting these groups. In addition to the economic pursuits apart, endeavours will not create ecological resource exhaustion and pauperisation of the region. Thus, all economic development, through various projects and schemes, a new relationship - a network will foster the groups through involvement and participation. The nature of economic enterprises, thus encompass not only the utilisation of the existing ecology through the traditional infrastructures but with science and technology to show a promise of prosperity and affluence. In all these projects and schemes, meant for the groups, tons of money has been spent. But sustainable benefits have not been achieved out of these. The implementing authorities and the planners spend the money on good purposes for which receipts and utilisation certificates are available all the time. This is a satisfactory state of affairs.

6

Education and Development

I

The independence of India ushered in new vistas for the downtrodden, and it has been repeatedly proclaimed that education for all is a must, as education is the only means by which all sorts of developmental processes can be visualised and as the people will be in a position to overcome the insurmountable difficulties in and around them, through awakening and creating their awareness. This will shake them of from an age-old stupor and anachronistic behaviour. When the educational facilities are extended to the tribals they will articulate with the new and existing system of social situations and, consequently, new facilities will be made available to them by which their stereotyped way of life will surely change. The British Education Policy was typical, limited and extended to certain groups of fortunate people only. The ultimate aim of this education was the happy breeding ground of clerks who were to support the British rule. In spite of all this, there were variations here and there, Gandhiji's Basic Education Policy was to make an individual a self-reliant, self-sufficient and a harbourer of patriotic zeal; Tagore's education policy of the new realisation was an exceptional example in this direction. Of course, Lokanayak's (Jaiprakash Narayan) attitude to education policy had no experimental background and do not clearly spell out the scheme, though he was wholeheartedly against the traditional system of the then prevailing British educational pattern. However, a picture relating to general literacy of the people of India with reference to tribes is reflected in Table 6.1.

Table 6.1
Total Literacy of the Indian Population

Year	*Total Literacy Percentage*	*S.T. Literacy Percentage*
1931	7.50	0.75
1961	28.29	8.54
1971	29.45	11.30
1981	36.23	16.35

Source : *Census of India-1981.*

Independence has acclerated the pace of the rate of education as it has been given some priority. Besides, the Government of India decided to exempt payment of educational fees upto the primary standard initially and this undoubtedly resulted in the gradual increase in the number of students *vis-a-vis* literacy. Though at the very inception there were many difficulties, including building up of infrastructures, recruitment of suitable teachers, communication facilities, accommodation of the staff, medium of instruction and many other ilks, we find a picture that reflects the school system, barring the other ways of adult education. A detailed analysis of the tribal education will reveal the following pictures shown in Table 6.2.

Table 6.2

Progress of Tribal Education

(Classes read : No. in lakh)

Year	*I-IV*	*VI-VIII*	*IX & X*
1955-56	10.45	1.24	0.54
1970-71	24.63	3.79	1.71
1980-81	46.60	7.72	2.66
1983-84	54.00	10.00	3.06

(Classes read : No. in lakh)

Source : Government of India Data.

This undoubtedly reflects the picture of tribal education, in general, because the tribal communities in India have a distinctive socio-economic background. Naturally, the question of the Primtive Tribal Groups should reveal a gloomier picture. However, Basic Edcation of Gandhiji was initiated in many places of the country and, with these, Ashram facilities in providing food, uniform, etc. were made only to the students of a section of the P.T.G. along with the trained teachers. They are to be oriented and this pattern has little deviation from the State education pattern. Some of the educational institutions are now run by voluntary organisations in different parts of the country where dedicated and committed teachers available. Besides, in order to supplement these, there are training facilities extended to the teachers and gradually the Tribal Welfare Department as well as the State Education Department also thought it necessary to establish some schools in the tribal dominated areas. But sometimes the medium of instruction and the curriculum have not been modified along with the seasonal variations of the school timings. Infrastructures, communication and accommodation problems etc. of course constitute the prime concern of the authorities. In West Bengal, specially for the tribals, there were provisions of Ashram facilities only for the students belonging to the tribal groups, but these were upto secondary level, i.e., upto VI-VIII standard. There are a few such schools located at different parts of the State. In spite of the realisation of the problems of the more backward tribal groups, no positive response was evinced by the State Goverment till 1963 when an All India Conference was held at the old Parliament House in Delhi under the Presidentship of Late Lal Bahadur Shastri, the then Home Minister of India, attended by the Late Prime Minister Jawaharlal Nehru and Shri U.N. Dhebar. This Conference was mainly meant to surface the problems of the Ex-Criminal Tribes, re-named as 'De-Notified Tribes'. In India, there were then 117 such communities of which the Lodhas were one. Late Prof. P.R. Sen represented the Harijan Sevak Sangh and Prof. P.K. Bhowmick (the author) of the Calcutta University, both of whom were recommended by the State Government, and were supposed to deal with the problems of the Lodhas as they were closely associated with the Lodhas problems. In course of the deliberations, Prof. Bhowmick insisted on the point of socialising the Lodha children and to articulate them from the existing middle-class norm and, for this purpose, Ashram facilities should be extended upto the Primary level. The Lodhas, who constitute one of the groups of the ex-criminal tribes, should be paid particular attention if the Government want to improve their lot. Instantly, under the instruction of the late Prime Minister, one Ashram Hostel was set up to be built by the Samaj Sevak Sangh of which Prof. Bhowmick is the founder-father. This organisation is located in an area under Narayangarh P.S. where the Lodhas constitute the majority population and the Centre was supposed to tackle their problems with a scientific approach. It is better to examine the actual educational situation of the Primitive Tribal Groups who are located at different parts of the State, having distinctive socio-cultural life. The cases of the Toto, Birhor, Lodha and the Kharia have been discussed separately and examined from a close range the nature of their educational facilities along with the critical evaluation in the following sections.

II

Among the tribals, the expansion of State level educational system upto the Primary level was very much limited. Of course, some of the tribals had the advantage of school education in a comparatively better way than others, when the group of the people were within the fold of Christianity. But in the isolated, sylvan surroundings where these tribals live, practically no systematic modern education had penetrated. There were lack of facilities and scope no doubt, and even where the Primary Schools were located, a system of regularity was not maintained. In respect of these Primitive Tribal Groups, like the Toto, Birhor and the Lodha/Kharia, this type of endeavour is actually non-existent. Of course, there are certain exceptions to the rule - the Lodhas got some opportunities when they live in the vicinity of the caste people and they are in a slow process of interacting with them. But deliberate attempt on the part of any organisation or even by the Government was not at all perceptible. The cases of the Totos, who live in claustrophobic isolation of the hill slopes, sandwitched in between by the river Torsa and a gorging rivulet, had the advantage of getting the attention of the

Lutheran World Service who practically set up schools, a Primary Health Centre and a cottage Industry, only to improve the condition of the Totos. However, in the pre-independence days, there was no attempt on the part of anybody to spread literacy among these groups of people and, even after independence, the attempt has not at all been remarkable. Sporadic attempts to impart literacy, especially among the Lodhas, by some individuals were made. Late Prof. P.R. Sen, attempted to open a branch of Harijan Sevak Sangh at Auligeria (P.S. Jhargram) and with the help of the authorities in the Education Department, Government of West Bengal opened a Pre-Basic School and also a Basic School upto Class-V standard, sometime in 1952. Bharat Sevashram Sangh at Pukuria (under Jhargram P.S.) organised a Primary level school and at Daharpur a Junior Basic School was set up by Prof. Bhowmick where he started some welfare schemes among the Lodhas. Gradually, Prof. Bhowmick organised a few adult education centres at distant areas in Midnapur and also *Khadi* work in some villages only to bring the Lodhas in touch with the other groups of people. Birkar, Dihipur, Kadamdiha, Sankaridanga are some of the villages having such work centres. Ultimately, the then School Board of Midnapur sanctioned these schools as one-teacher Special Cadre Primary Schools. These are located in the Lodha concentrated areas and these enabled the Lodhas to have a school of their own. However, approval of an Ashram Hostel for the Primary level students was received for the development of the Lodhas as they belonged to the denotified criminal tribes. Similarly, at Ranibandh, one Ashram Hostel was approved by the Government to be built through the District Welfare Officer for the benefit of the Kharias. Initially, the nature of extension of financial grants were made under the following heads :

1. Construction of building

unit for 20 students. : Rs. 20,000.
2. Meal charges : Rs. 40x12x20 per head.
3. Misc., haircutting, K.oil, soap etc. : Rs. 0.85 paisa per head.
4. Sports & games annually : Rs. 100 (total).
5. Clothing for one year : Rs. 40. per head.
6. Medicine for all : Rs. 100.
7. Agricultural training (1 year) : 200.-
8. Worker's wage per month : Rs. 50x12 = Rs. 600.
9. Helper's wage per month : Rs. 30x12 = Rs. 360.
10. Supdt's pay per month : Rs. 100.

A sum of Rs. 3,000 was sanctioned for the purchase of utensils, blankets etc. for the inmates initially. These were the monetary provisions for the Ashram Hostels which were set up by the Government of India and this type of Unit was started in 1964 after the Conference held at Delhi for the amelioration of the lot of the Lodhas. In addition, some educational facilities were also extended to them from time to time, as and when situation demanded and Government fund were syphoned. All these attempts appear to be of exploratory nature and it so happened that many more correctional or experimental provisions could have been started to accelerate the speed by overcoming the snags of all types. But it did not happen so, nor were they evaluated or alternatives sought for by the Government.

III

The literacy rate of the Totos was 9.05 in 1989. It changed however due to certain amount of sincere endeavour taken by the voluntary organisations, like Bharat Mahajati Mondali and the Lutheran World Service initially and, later on, by the Tribal Welfare Department. A report (Dhali : 1987) reflected that out of 539 persons (227 male and 265 female) only 44 males and 3 females are considered to be literate, calculating 8.17% literacy. The Christian missionaries upto 1968 encouraged only 7 Toto students to be regularly present in School. Later, this number rose to 26 in 1969. Situation began to change for the better again in 1979 when the number increased to 61. Residential quarters were built in Totopara and this enabled the teachers to take interest in the matter of spread of education among the Totos and ultimately this interaction has had a definite impact on the life-style of the said tribe. A few students went out of their narrow environs and at least one passed the Madhyamik Examination. L.W.S. simultaneously arranged to start Adult Education centres and for this purpose the same mission engaged two teachers - one male and one female. The said missionary organisation also started one Junior High School in 1979. The same report (Dhali) shows that 15 boys and 2 girls were reading in different Secondary classes outside the villages, especially in Madarihat and Cooch Behar.The Junior High School is named Dhanapati Toto Memorial School (1979). The State Government Education Department took over its management in 1982. No Ashram facilities have been extended for the students of the Junior High School.

Again, in six wards, six adult education centres have been started. Out of these, only 4 centres are running at present, but the attendance of the students in these centres is very irregular. The teachers of the Adult Education Centres are paid Rs. 100 per month by the Government Education (Social) Department, West Bengal. In 1982, a Rural Library was organised by which the people of the locality interact with others. Of course, this is an apology for a real Rural Library, for the books are few and far between here. But it subscribes a few dailies and some periodicals for the use of the indoor readers of the library. Two Toto boys have been assigned the charge of looking after the Library. Here, infrastructures are there, but the lack of initiative on the part of the members is a great malaise which will be apparent even to a casual onlooker. The Ashram Hostel for the Totos has 30 seats, but at the time of inspection they showed the scribe a record of 24 and actually all those were not present. This is meant for the boys only. There is no Special Superintendent and the Headmaster of the School works as the Superintendent of the Hostel. He frankly admitted that the amount sanctioned by the Government (Rs. 100 per month) at that time, is not attractive enough to attract anybody for this job. Besides, the release of the grant is extremely tortuous. Naturally, irregularity prevails. The cook and the lady-helper generally look after them as they belong to the same community.

IV

The Birhors, a gathering-hunting group of people, are practically found to live in three villages on the Bengal-Bihar border. Our survey reveals the literacy rate of this group to be 12.73%. This is due to the smallness of their number available in the locality. Of course, attempts were made earlier to extend education among the Birhors by the Government through some welfare activities. As a result, one rehabilitation colony named Bhupati Palli was started where some Birhor families from two neighbouring villages were encouraged to live. They were given housing facilities, including a school which used to be a Store House in the past, for keeping some implements purchased for the welfare of the Birhors by the Government. No hostel building in the form of an Ashram Hostel has been started for the Birhors. But in the vicinity there is a voluntary organisation named 'Kalyan Ashram' which runs a Balwadi, and a school upto Class-IV standard with Government recognition and grant. But no Ashram facilities have been extended to this organisation. Possibly, they have a different socio-political aim. The number of Birhor children who read in the school are shown in the table below :

Table 6.3
Birhor Children Reading in The School

Sex	*Class I-IV*	*Class V-VII*	*Total*
Male	13	1	14
Famale	7	-	7
Total	20	1	21

V

The Lodhas were treated as a Criminal Tribe before the revocation of the Act in 1952. Naturally, many more hostile attitudes of the neighbouring public and the administrators were hurled at them. Practically, the Lodhas were never encouraged to get schooling in the pre-Independent India. No efforts were made to educate them by anybody and at the same time they were reluctant to attend any school. But, after Independence, some facilities were extended to them. The mentality of the Lodha Children was not to have any schooling even if school is at a stone's throw from their residence. Besides, their parents did not like it too. A thorough survey (Bhowmick : 1963) made in this regard indicates that the literacy rate of the Lodhas in two distinctive zones of Midnapur district - one jungle covered and isolated zone of Jhargram-Narayangarh-Gopiballabpur-Jamboni and -Binpur blocks is 0.29%, whereas the other zone which is more associated with the caste groups, like Midnapur (north and south) subdivisions where Lodhas have the advantages of interacting with the neighbouring Caste Hindu people had the literacy rate of 2.59%. This very clearly indicates that interaction with the neighbouring groups prompted them to a better literacy rate. But a recent survey indicates 10.96% literacy rate which shows an increase undoubtedly over the rate from Bhowmick's study. This is due to certain factors and steps initiated by the Government about the total eradication of illiteracy (in 1990-91) will add a new dimension to it. It has been stated that some limited voluntary efforts were made at different Lodha concentrated zones by a few individuals associated with some voluntary organisations. They had practically to steer clear the difficulties for the spread of education. Besides, a few 'One teacher - Special Cadre Primary Schools' were then set up by the District School Board (Education Department). Along with this, an Ashram Hostel Scheme was added after 1963 to many voluntary organisations having Basic Schools later on after CPI(M) came in power to Panchayat authorities, even before the Lodhas were declared as a Primitive Tribal Group (1980-81). It is said that the first Ashram Hostel meant for this de-notified Lodha community was given to the Samaj Sevak Sangh (popularly known as 'Bidisa' Project, and this organisation has started one Junior Basic School along with a Senior Basic School upto Class VIII standard). The Samaj Sevak Sangha had the privilege of doing welfare work and rehabilitation of the Lodha tribe sometime in 1963-64 and gradually raised grain-gola, multipurpose co-operative society not only for the benefit of the Lodhas alone but for the other tribal people also of the locality. Naturally, the attempt so far made for their welfare created confidence in the mind of the Lodhas and the people of other tribes. The administrators were very cuch satisfied with the work at 'Bidisa'. Consequently, in addition to the 20 existing seats, another set of 10 seats were sanctioned in the same establishment. As a result, the number of the Lodha seats for the boys became 30 sometime in 1965. Gradually, a few more Ashram Hostels have been sanctioned to some other organisations, though there was violation of the principles of sanctioning the Hostel to them, inasmuch as they are having no school under the management of its authorities. Again, at Bidisa, the Samaj Sevak Sangh had the advantage of a second Ashram Hostel in 1968, when the Lodha-Santal-Mahato riots broke out and a few Lodhas were killed and their villages set on fire. The then District Magistrate, Midnapur brought 20 Lodha childern from the riot torn areas of Jhargram and requested the authorities to accommodate them, and a separate unit was started to co-operate with the administration in such crucial circumstances. As usual, sum of Rs. 20,000 only was sanctioned for the second unit to construct the building. By this time, a good number of Ashram Hostels were sanctioned at different Lodha concentrated areas as a routine matter. Particulars of Ashram Hostels are given in Table 6.4.

Table 6.4

Ashram Hostels

Sl. No.	*Name and Particulars*	*Meant for and quota*	*Rupees Sanctioned*
	BOYS		
1.	Daharpur,Unit I, Samaj Sevak Sangh, Narayangarh, 1964	Boys : 30	20,000
2.	Pukuria Ashram Hostel, Bharat Sevashram Sangh, Jhargram, 1966	Boys : 25	20,000
3.	Badalpur Ashram Hostel, Unit-I, Do School, Sabang, 1969	Boys : 20	20,000
4.	Chaksahapur Ashram Hostel, Unit I, Debra, 1976	Boys : 30	25,000
5.	Daharpur Samaj Sevak Sangh	Boys : 20	20,000

	Unit II, 1968		
6.	Badalpur, Unit II, Sabong, 1969	Boys : Secondary level (Lodha & other tribals).	
7.	Chaksahapur, Debra Unit II, 1988	Boys : 30	No grant for institution.
8.	Krishnarakshitchak Ashram Hostel, Kharagpur, 1980	Boys : 30	50,000
9.	Singdui Ashram Hostel, Nayagram, 1980	Boys : 20	50,000/-
10.	Pathardahara, Nayagram, 1980.	Boys : 20	50,000
11.	Raiberia, Nayagram, 1980	Boys : 20	50,000
12.	Chandabila, Nayagram, 1980.	Boys : 20	50,000
13.	Satsol Ashram Hostel, Keshiary, 1986.	Boys : 30	50,000

GIRLS

1.	Daharpur Samaj Sevak Sangh, Narayangarh, 1970	Girls : 20	20,000
2.	Chaksahapur, Debra started to function in 1982.	Girls : 40	1,21,000/- (Sanctioned later more money to complete).
3.	Kharikamathani, Nayagram, 1980	Girls : 20	50,000
4.	Ramakrishna-Sarada Jhargram, 1983-84	Girls : 30	1,56,000

It may be mentioned here in this connection that most of the Ashram schools previously attached to a society had their own schools run by the same management, except at Chaksahapur. But the organisation failed though a huge sum of money was allotted to a young Lodha graduate of the locality for spearheading economic developments to his society which was registered one. Two units of Ashram hostel boys (30+30) were allotted to this organisation. Later on one unit of Ashram Girls' hostel (40) for which initially Rs. 1,21,000 was sanctioned and this was supposed to be misused. As a result, the scheme had to be abandoned for a long time. A further sum was released by the I.T.D.P. and T.W. Department for completion of the work and it was materialised through the Panchayat in 1988. It is now functioning. Five Ashram Hostels were started at Nayagram after the mass killing of the Lodhas in 1979 when 18 persons were killed by a few thousand angry men in broad daylight. Series of Lodha killings have been reported earlier due to hostile relationships of the Lodhas with other ethnic groups of the neighbourhood.

Assessing the Ashram Hostels different pictures emerge, of which 'Bidisa' is a model example by itself, as the authority here is in a position to run the Hostels independently when delayed grants are released. Regarding the Pukuria Ashram Hostel run by the Bharat Sevashram Sangha, Ramakrishna-Sarada Vidyapith (Jhargram) looked after by the Ramakrishna Mission and one Kharikamathani Girls' High School was allotted one unit of Girls' Hostel the authorities perform their work very satisfactorily. Another Bidisa-trained Lodha boy is in charge of Krishnarakshitchak Ashram Hostel (1980); his personal endeavour and initiatives in this regard are praiseworthy. Post-riot recommendation for the spread of education among the Lodhas at Singhdui is almost a flop. Similar is the case of Raiberia Hostel. Nobody was at the time of inspection. This indicates that nobody is to look after it. It is almost defunct. During the visit of the survey team, the Hostels under the Samaj Sevak Sangh, Bharat Sevashram Sangh, Ramakrishna-Sarada Vidyapith and Kharikamathani Girls' School were found on the rails and moving. Krishnarakshitchak showed an attendance of 22 students, Badalpur (Sabong) only 7 out of 20 and Pathardahara 13 (as it was closed for a long time). At the time of second visit of the team to the campus, the Superintendent in charge Chaksahapur group of hostels (3 units having 100 seats) confessed that very recently the Panchayat received a little sum as grant, just to keep pot boiling and hence the forlorn condition. They did not tell details as per advice of the Panchayat, Satsol under Keshiary P.S. reflects gloomy picture. It is run by the local Panchayat. They have been allotted 30 students, but the figure never goes beyond 14 or 15. Of course, practical difficulties are there and it is what it should be under the circumstances. At the time of visit to Chaksahapur where two units for boys (30 & 30). Hostels were sanctioned, only 41 students were found and 27 girls were shown out of the sanctioned quota of 40. Sanction of units one after another is due to a man who is an employee of the I.T.D.P. and managed to have the sanctioned money due to the priority of ethnic claim.

Again, for the encouragement to the Lodha students for the secondary standard of education, five High Schools in different areas of the Lodha belt have been recommended (1987) under the control of Zilla Parishad though the entire money was allotted to build up a campus just to fit the students in a blissful setting for their psycho-emotional problems.

Table 6.5

Schools Selected for Grants

1.	Ektal D.M.High School (Jhargram : Rs. 60,000)	:	for 20 students
2.	Baligeria S.C.High School, (Nayagram : Rs. 1,20,000)	:	for 40 students
3.	Gokulpur High School (Midnapur : Rs. 1,20,000)	:	for 40 students
4.	Santrapur High School (Keshiary : Rs. 1,20,000)	:	for 40 students
5.	Narayangarh High School (Narayangarh : Rs. 1,20,000)	:	for 40 students

Our scholars met the teaching staff and enquired about the Lodha students reading in these schools. At almost all the places, the buildings are under construction or are about to be completed. Ektal School shows a register containing names of the Lodha boys, and they expect to make up the lee-way existing till now. The Baligeria High School authority and also the Sabhapati is Sri Nalini Ranjan Mahato, a very energetic and sincere person. The roll strength of the Lodha students here is 24 and other students will be accommodated in due course as and when the building will be completed. The Gokulpur High School has yet to see their buildings completed and the teacher-in-charge claims that they will get Lodha boys here. Similar is also the case with the School at Santrapur under Keshiary P.S. The Narayangarh High School has been given one Unit of 40 Lodha students. Previously, they were given one Unit of the Tribal Hostel which is being used by the other and the face of the Hostel at this place is in complete disarray. This is mostly due to influence of the local political party who get these sanctioned. Allotment for the spread of education (1988-89), for both the Lodha and the Kharia students, in the following schools/places have been earmarked by the I.T.D.P. :

Table 6.6

School Receiving Latest Grants

1.	Ujan High School for 30 boys (Lodha Primary 30 students)	:	Rs. 1,50,000
2.	Chaksahapur Girl's High School Unit II for 30 girls.	:	Rs. 1,50,000
3.	Dubra High School, Jamboni for 30 boys (Lodha) Primary (1990-91)	:	Rs. 1,50,000
4.	Jhargram Block for 30 boys (Lodha : 1990-91) [No site selection has been made].	:	Rs. 1,50,000
5.	Ramakrishna-Sarada Vidyapith Jhargram for 30 Lodha girls of all classes. IInd Unit (1988-89).	:	Rs. 1,56,900
6.	Udalchua, Binpur II for 30 boys (Kharia) (1988-89).	:	Rs. 1,00,000
7.	Silda Girls' High School for 30 girls (Kharia) Secondary level (1988-89).	:	Rs. 1,30,000

In this connection, series of complaints against Chaksahapur organisation having groups of hostels for the Lodhas both boys and girls, were submitted to all the responsible authorities, including the Sabhadhipati. In consequence, the grant was withheld temporarily and the tragedy of tragedies is that it has been released without a thorough probe on a later date. They have 100 students (boys 60, girls 40) and then another girl unit of 30 students sanctioned (1991). Their performance is not at all satisfactory and an investigation into the matter is a crying need as to how the hostels are being sanctioned and why though grants are being released late all the time and the Panchayat or organisation in charge of running hostels has no schools under their management and the progress is yet to be proved. It is said that one Lodha employee is interested as it was in his own village. Schemes for fishery and dairy were allotted there with heavy amount leading to complete failure. It is said that while sanction of first girls Ashram Hostel the money was diverted by the organiser to purchase a truck for business with an idea to build up asset. Later on, Government took action and fresh grant released to complete girl unit (40) first one.

The Kharias have been extended educational benefits. Before they were considered at P.T.G. (bracketted with the Lodhas), one Ashram Hostel was started at Ranibandh (Bankura) under the management the Tribal Welfare Department, and their attempt has been satisfactory. Very recently another Ashram Hostel building has been completed at Banspahari, Jhargram, which is attached to the High School by the T.W. Department. There are many enthusiastic and sincere teachers, but it is not functioning. If proper attempts are made by the authorities, it can yield good results as the Kharia villages are near the school. However, in the case of the Kharias the matters are more disorganised due to lack of devoted social workers and sincere teachers. Problems are there, no doubt, but these are to be tackled and the people should not be allowed to plot under no circumstances.

VII

Nevertheless, it has been proved that education takes a backseat among ther Primitive Tribal Groups, as all these people have varied problems of their own. The Totos living in isolated pockets are being exploited unscrupulously by the dominant Nepalis and other caste people who encroached upon their benefits in a slow degree. Their medium of instruction is Bengali which is rather difficult for the Toto children to learn. Here, some alternative need to be suggested. Everywhere the release of grants take place at a snail's pace. It was Rs. 40 initially but in course of time slowly stages by stages it has been increased to Rs. 150 (since May 1990-91). The other items that the children need are not upto the desired standard. The Hostel Superintendent gets Rs. 200 only per month, whereas in other States they get all the perquisites in addition like that of a Primary School Teacher. Similar is the case with the Hostel cook who gets Rs. 100 only. The school for the Birhors is yet to start functioning, at least some provisions should be made to accommodate a few Birhor children in the Ramakrishna Mission School at Purulia. The authorities are very serious in the matter, and the delay in releasing the grants for this may be avoided. In any case, these children have different psycho-emotional attachments and their guardians are not very keen to allow them to stay in the Hostels when these children become a little older and physically fit to be engaged as cow-herd boys in the nearby villages. This helps them augment their slender income and subsidise the economic condition of the families. The Lodha, neglected as they are for years, and ultimately made pawns in the hands of the receivers of stolen property obtained from anti-social activities, as also cadres in the hands of the political leaders in their power game, are the real havenots and victims of unimaginable exploitations. As a result, series of carnages due to change of receivers took place previously in the Lodha areas. It is true that the problems of the Lodhas are of different nature. They have not been understood properly by anybody with sympathy and seriousness with the passage of time this has left in their mind some cracks and fissures which are very difficult to plug. Various alternatives could have been suggested to the administration but nobody is there to touch them with a pair of tongs even, and these are willy-nilly glossed over and neglected. For instance, the Ashram Hostel for the Lodha boys has been running limpingly, a secret conspiracy is there and this will be amply clear to all the discerning minds. Take an example; to run the Units at Chaksahapur, at least the organisers require Rs. 150 for each of the 100 students per month (100 students is the maximum quota arranged for them by the authorities through another 30 seats for girls have been allotted) which comes to Rs. 15,000 per month at the minimum at present and for three months the figure will be Rs. 15,000 x 3 = Rs. 45.000, if they want to keep the flag flying. Is it possible for the Panchayat organisation with their small means to bear this expenditure? The same organisation, it has been noticed, were given successive grants to complete the one unit of Girls' Hostel (having 40 seats). The result for the Girls' Hostel has yet to be examined, because only they were allowed to get green signal and none else. But the same organisation had shown favour for the second time, for these 40 girls only in that Unit. They had no other facilities - neither a school of their own nor any other alternative arrangement or even any other visible advantages in or around their locality. All the cases of the Ashram Hostels are more or less the same - grants released without examining the output or the performance of the institution. It is also said that one employee in the ITDP office arranged to allot one Ashram Hostel to the village of his first-wife's father at Satsol (Keshiary), just to placate his anger.

The Lodhas require a special treatment - a special timing for their school hours and they need to be interlaced with the regional population through participation and encouragement. In this respect, the Samaj Sevak Sangh can claim to be more helpful, as many graduates have come out from there (of whom two are Lodhas) and they often organise many functions and celebrations in tendem with the local people using the big campus. But the authority expressed, in writing, to the District Magistrate and the Sabhadhipati and S.O.T.W. to withdraw the permission as they did not get even a single paise for the repair work of the buildings, though they were initially granted Rs. 20,000 under this head, for each of the three Units at the time of their opening. This sort of discrimination wounded the feelings of the organisers of all the institutions which are having good record in the All India scene (Lodha students went to Delhi when Indira Gandhi was the Prime Minister for All India Conference) and the organisers sent the Lodha students in many other All India Competitions.

However, all these can be assessed once more to bring home the matter. In this connection, it may be said that selection of the place in many cases do not justify the cause; when money is available, the children are herded and brought like poultry birds and at other times they go elsewhere. Only a few reputed organisations have the capacity to bear the burden of advancing money for running the Hostels. Of coures in a few cases money is being released in Tribal Welfare Department and in some cases by I.T.D.P.

This indicates that the authorities are not serious about improving the condition of these people and never think it worthwhile to consult with others, who are experts in the field. In this regard, it may be said that this year (1990-91) some maintenance (food and others) grant has been released after the last October, 1990 to some organisers. As such, how they are expected to maintain the Hostels? This is one scenario of the welfare endeavour for these downtrodden people. The other picture is about the communities themselves, specially the Primitive Tribal Groups. Many aspects of the people and the children's psychology are being neglected in various ways. If the problems are to be tackled adequately, steps should be taken in the right direction as it is out of the Central Government money that these are running and no profit motive should find any place in anybody's mind in the name of the downtrodden, keeping them denied and deprived of their essentially basic needs, like education, health, good drinking water, shelter etc.

7

Health, Hygiene and Sanitation

I

The tribal communities, like all other homosapiens, live in an environment which leave profound impact on their health. Certain areas are prone to certain types of disqualifications or defects. Sometimes good drinking water is not available there and the people have to suffer for lack of it without being able to take any remedial measure. Even sufficient amount of water is not obtainable to take a bath or wash clothes and utensils. Besides, their worldview becomes narrower and due to inhumanly style of living and interacting they make. They are also not aware of the types of diseases and the modern scientific discoveries to combat them. In their blissful ignorance, therefore, these people name many of their failures, difficulties, illnesses etc. as the effects of some wrath of the supernatural agencies - the spirits which create the troubles, illnesses that even lead to death of the afflicted person. Of course, we cannot attribute these only to the tribal people, but also to many other caste people. Naturally, the people will try their utmost to pacify the hostile spirits, ghosts of the dead or perhaps the punishment inflicted on them due to breach of some taboos. But nowadays, many modern facilities have come to their door-steps, especially in the matter of getting good drinking water. In this regard, there may be some constraints here and there, but still some facilities about health care and treatment have undoubtedly become easily available just for a song. Thus, the people are subjected or exposed to such salutary conditions. As a result, a mental make up through some kind of socialisation processes are growing. Yet, the traditionalism hovers over the tribal scenario- the difficulties of transport facility to the hospital or to the Medical Centre. But magicians, sorcerers, witch doctors, shamans and priests are there to help them in their bizzare situations, fairly and squarely, performing certain rites and rituals, ceremonies and worships or sometimes being oath-bound to propitiate the deities after the recovery through divine dispensation, and there the propitiatory worship custom comes in. On the other hand, there is no denying the fact that physician or even quack doctors are not available in and around many tribal hamlets; Primary Health Centres are there but without any medicine or even the medicare personnel. Naturally, therefore, the attempts with good intentions of the Government or the voluntary organisations involved in social welfare work come to their help and succour. On this backdrop, we find both the above systems functioning side by side- belief in the supernatural power as a disease creating force, illness and some other troubles, and the belief in the modern medical help. It is obvious that the tribal people use some medicinal herbs and plants and experimented both by the *Ayurvedic* practitioners and the researchers who are trying to glean into the matter for utilising them in an effective way. However, a mixed picture has filled the panorama of the tribal scene in respect of health and hygiene. Besides, housing and sanitation problems cannot be brushed aside while discussing the question of health of the tribals, in general, and that of the Primitive Tribal Groups, in particular. Along with these, the need for the minimum requirement of wearing apparel cannot also be overlooked, as all these are associated with the health and hygiene of the tribals. Above all, the impoverished condition, i.e., their poor and uncertain economy, lack of education in respect of health and hygiene and sanitation, want of availability of good drinking water, communication facility and lack of the Primary Health Centre personnel stand in the way of the development of the people, as a whole.

II

We have seen that after Independence some facilities have been extended to the tribal people and, in spite of that some groups have been treated as Primitive Tribal Groups. We have already dwelt on the background information of these groups systematically concerning the nature of their physical setting and the way the facilities have been extended to them, not only through the general welfare work but also after these people were categorised as P.T.G. since 1980-81. In spite of these ameliorative schemes and projects for them, we can categorically say that the attempts to provide good drinking water from masonry wells has not been successful.

The Totos living in the hill slopes could not utilise the water as it is beyond their reach. From the very beginnig stage of the welfare work among these groups, many attempts were made by which they could get good drinking water. Many kinds of skin diseases developed by these groups of people were the result of their shabby and unclean habits and the stinks of their body attract even a casual onlooker to these people. Though there are series of complaints against the contractors, who were responsible for many ills, as per the Government version, in the matter of supplying good water at the Totopara, nothing could be done to set things right. The Lutheran World Service took initiative to open a Health Centre at Totopara and they tried to attract the people there to make the fullest use of it. This depends mostly on the nature of health education imparted on the Totos and develop a habit of cleanliness, provided plenty of water and clothes are there for them to change and a habit of better maintenance of health through clean atmosphere is imbibed.

The case of the Birhors is different. Some water is supplied to them from ring wells and these people have become accustomed to the use of drinking pure water. In addition, there is a water reservoir in the vicinity which can be utilised by them for bathing and washing purposes. But the fundamental difficulties that immediately attract the attention of the people are their penurious condition and the unavailability of adequate number of wearing apparels to enable them to change and wash the dirty ones in time. They are also lacking in the habit of observing cleanliness by washing their mouth and body. The general approach of the Government in this regard is very well intentioned, but the training and socialisation of these tribal people cannot be done by the so-called contractors or the Government officials who dominate the scene without the actual volition of the people concerned.

The case of the Lodhas is somewhat better, as they are in the habit of living side by side with the other caste group people. Though some of them are victims of abject poverty, and are numerically small, their desire to copy the caste people and to have a better health and sanitary condition is clearly visible. On the contrary, the Lodhas living in the far away places insulated in between by the jungles, bereft of proper communication facilities, are not drawn towards the bigger societies around them. All this are attributable to their poor economic condition and the nature of lukewarm support to the welfare schemes undertaken for these groups, through the Panchayat organisations.

More precarious existence awaits the Kharias, who live in comparatively isolated areas and in a rugged terrain. The welfare works proposed to be done in the form of digging of wells etc. are not at all satisfactory. Dug wells have been sanctioned for them but those could not materialise or are done half way, indicating clearly that the people are not aware of the welfare motive of the Government on the one hand and the lack of articulation, on the other. The modern educational system have put them in an extreme difficulty, which can only be appreciated by a casual visitor, who has an inkling about the Government grants and their likes. This group suffers perennial disadvantages and they adjust themselves with the situation without a murmur to anybody, because insufficiency and ill-health are constant companions in the life of these people. There is no scope of complaining or questioning on the part of the people, and no assurances are given to them by the officers or the Panchayat representatives to allay their grievances, worries and anxieties. The local Government functionaries also do not assuage their bitter feelings of frustration in this respect. All this-taken together, and coupled with their ignorance, has put them in an unenviable difficult situation. While examining some cases, our researchers did not find existence of a single item of the sanctioned articles supplied to them by the Government which indicates utter failure of the scheme. This naturally leads to suspicion about the sincerity and earnestness of the donor and the donee.

Of course, Shri D.Das, the Project Officer, Jhargram understood the problem and had sanctioned a fresh grant to complete one or two such incomplete wells sanctioned, through the contractors selected by the Panchayats, which proved in the final analysis to be accountable for their lapses. However, a survey (1989-90) in connection with the prevalence of diseases has been made and the results recorded which will be found in Table 7:1

Table 7.1

Disease Pattern

(Total in percentage)

Sl. No.	*Name of Diseases*	*Tribes* Toto	*Birhor*	*Lodha*	*Kharia*
1.	**Influenza**	40.8	23.3	30.2	12.37
2.	**Typhoid**	3.6	1.4	5.6	1.1
3.	Malaria	7.3	5.3	25.4	51.6
4.	Cough	9.4	5.0	12.3	3.1
5.	Blood Dysentry	4.3	3.6	2.1	1.6
6.	Hooping Cough	0.7	0.3	2.0	-
7.	Diarrhoea	8.7	14.2	11.1	8.0
8.	Jaundice	1.4	2.0	3.7	1.9
9.	Skin Diseases	38.9	21.1	10.0	13.2
10.	Arthritis	1.4	3.7	5.2	7.2

III

It has been indicated that due to lack of sufficient water supply, some of the vector borne diseases prevail, but these people have their own remedial systems, as indicated earlier, through some specialised persons like the magician, sorcerer, shaman and priest. Along side this many of them found to wear talisman, amulet etc. for prophylectic purposes, as well as for curative measures against all sorts of physical and mental ailments. But the basic difficulties in respect of health and hygiene are to:

(i) provide good drinking water;

(ii) acquaint them with the Primary Health Centres;

(iii) acquaint them with the health guides who will take initiative, regular survey and report to the nearby Health Centre.

Enquiries revealed that the Lodhas badly need health, education, maternity services and the post-natal treatments. They were found to bury the placenta and after-birth waste matters near the hearth. The Kharias put these in the corner of the courtyard where rain water drops during the rainy season, in order to avoid the wandering spirits to cause spread of child-diseases and death.

This once vigorous tribal stock began to degenerate due to their persisting poverty. It is a fact that most of them never use mosquito-nets or pillows. Even during the winter, most of them do not possess a good wrapper. Instead, specially among the Birhors, Lodhas or the Kharias, they dig up a fire place where faggots, firewood and other fuels are kept burning for the whole night just to keep themselves warm and combat the biting cold.

Even most of these tribal groups have only one cloth to cover their body. More precarious is the condition of their women folks who are found sometimes to wear half of a cloth and dry up the remaining portion either in the sun or in the wind. Under such circumstances of chill penury, it is futile to consider about their health and hygiene. Naturally, therefore, to improve their health and hygiene, it is the a priori condition to bring about a condition of stable in their income and impart thereafter education on the basis of which they can afford to have the facilities of modern medicines. At the same time, Mobile Medical Units can be started for them and they should be provided with good drinking water with which they can prevent the water-communicable diseases. Inoculation and vaccination against epidemic diseases along with First-Aid facilities should be brought to their door-steps on the basis of which we can find the people in a better condition.

All in all, the health and hygienic conditions of these groups are not at all satisfactory at present due to the problems enunciated above.

Part Three

CONCLUSION AND SUGGESTIONS

8

CONCLUSION AND SUGGESTIONS

I

It is a patent fact that 'Primitivism persists, side by side, as an adjunct to modern society'. Thus most of the Primitive Tribal Groups categorised as such have till date the archaic style of living in spite of the respective welfare projects pursued for their benefits by the Government since Independence. Successive evaluations of the conditions of the tribal communities of our country made by many teams of experts, their observations and suggestions convey that they are at the 'lowest rung' of the societal ladder, even among the tribal groups and therefore they merit special attention.

The Government of India declared 74 communities to date as 'Primitive Tribal Groups' or P.T.G., though some of them live in more than one state and counted more than once. Most of these groups still consider themselves a part of nature or the environment in which they live and have developed a world-view of reciprocity with nature that can be called transcendental naturalism or 'Supernaturalism'. In course of such interactional processes their behavioural pattern, mental attitude and even the societal rules have had to conform to their traditions and, we sometimes find that they blindly obey these patterns. These societies have once enjoyed the bounties of nature - as blissful pagans - but due to historical ups and downs, brutal and inhumanistic interactions or inroads with the hostile forces or seemingly scheming groups, they had to face many eventualities and in consequence had to face unfortunate situations and varied disadvantages. All these hint at a state of affairs which is aptly called a *culture of poverty*. In this connection, it is to be noted that these groups have been relatively less efficient in the matters of their food production and have no proper technology or education to control and utilise the resources properly. Their persisting ill-health and the like gyrate them all the while. All these have lowered the levels of socio-cultural integration with other communities in and around them, dragging them through a vicious atmosphere of misunderstanding, distrust and occasional fits of violence as we have seen recently in the case of the Lodhas. Communities like the Totos, a mongoloid group of people, numerically very thin, living on the slopes of the Himalayan *Tarai*, the Birhor, a very primitive group in the border areas of Bengal and Bihar (main concentration being in Bihar), and the Lodhas, in Bihar, Orissa and West Bengal, the Kharias who have been bracketed with the Lodha, (though these two groups assert themselves, by a common term *Savara or Sabbar*, just to identify themselves with the name in the *Puranic* literatures as an ancient tribe called 'Savara' are examples of marginal communities. The Kharias merited such facilities as are given to the Primitive Tribal Groups, because their socio-economic condition demands such consideration, although their name has been omitted, from the list of West Bengal (PTG) very recently.

On such a backdrop, a critical analysis of the culture of these groups has been made. The nature of welfare activities leading to development and for minimising the prevailing social and economic distances and then welfare schemes and projects since Independence have been examined. The welfare activities were expected to be accelerated greatly because of the vigorous actions taken by the Government following the inclusion of these groups at P.T.G, since 1980-81. The schemes, projects and the nature of benefits to the beneficiaries have been discussed item-wise to present a picture of the situation. In conclusion, we agree with the observations of G. Balagopala, the then Deputy Commissioner, Jalpaiguri (1982) and Vice-Chairman of the Jalpaiguri Tribal Advisory Committee in respect of the Totos which is applicable *mutatis mutandis* to the other tribes as well.

II

This evaluation report tries to indicate the inadequacy of the implementing machinery on the one hand and lack of experience, kid-glove attitude of the planners for reaching at the root of their cultural constraints, on the other. As a result, one positive break-through could be made in the matter and no perceptible dent could be made to fathom the depth of the existing penurious condition of the people concerned living scattered in different socio-economic milieu, different degrees of interactions in the state. The net result is that the poor became poorer. Some fortunate tribesmen with some accessibility to grant-sanctioning authorities forever, gained and could acquire some power and pelf from the resources channelised by the Central Government. No viable plan suitable to these groups of people as a whole has properly been drawn to speed up the development process. Most of the plans already drawn are faulty, misdirected, and fail to anticipate the future difficulties of the communities. These often raise doubts over the seriousness of the social objectives. Therefore, it is necessary why a meaningful programme for the development, identifying the problems of the groups and anticipating the nature arising out of those programmes, should be clearly thought out if necessary drastically changing the existing ones. This approach seems to be conspicuous by its absence in formulating and implementing the plans. Naturally, the repeated failures benumbered their spirits and piled up problem after problem of these people. This being the case, the target groups turned into 'dole' receiving beggars at the hands of the so-called authorities, who supposedly represent our democratic Government. These representatives do not seem to have neither a clear thinking, nor any definite idea about the developmental progress and welfare - most of them even do not understand the intents of purpose of the programmes, or over the applicability and viability of the plan strategies. In consequence, the target groups remain steeped in poverty, backwardness, disillusionment and ignorance. They are voiceless and perplexed in tackling their little problems by themselves. Their fate are being moulded by some other people largely of alien origin, wielding power, but no idea of real development or welfare to make the target groups self-reliant and capable. While discussing various economy revamping projects and schemes, it has been very clearly stated that many items of the welfare programmes are useless, e.g., the offering the fruit-bearing trees, allocation of bullocks and goats, etc. coupled with dishonesty by the implementing organisations. Just because money has been sanctioned, it was thought necessary to spend to and it provide utilisation certificates, be it conducive to the target groups or not. This is a negative approach to the developmental schemes/projects which, in all fairness, should have been avoided by any honest person. This lop-sided policy of giving meaningless priorities to unimportant items are the bane to the actual work and, as such, no esoteric benefits could be achieved out of these half-hearted endeavours. Many items were sanctioned for the target groups and as proof to purchasing them vouchers have been kept as bonafide audited reports, but there is no trace of any of them, in reality. Even if there was existence of some, they did not make any difference to the people as those were of least or no use to them. Hence the lukewarm response from them in some places, money for digging wells was sanctioned, but no well was found in actual existence. In the case of granting money to the 'Printex Works' at Jhargram (Appendix), the same is the story. The above examples are illustrative and not exhaustive. But here we must give the devil his due. There are a few cases where a wee-bit of economic benefit or other responses have resulted from such attempts, but for it no development agency can be praised, as the forest grows without the look-see of the Forest Department.

Attempts to educate these people have proved a grand failure. Even, in spite of public protest on the activities of a particular organisation at Chaksahapur P.S. Debra in the district of Midnapur, grant (for the Lodha) has been again released to the same, proving the presence of the vested interests and the whims and caprices of the local politicians, whereas cases of voluntary organisations, viz. Samaj Sevak Sangha, Bharat Sevashram Sangha of

Midnapur, Kharika mathani Girls' School which was ignored.

In this connection it is to be noted that in order to evaluate a development or welfare activity, one must consider the socio-economic landscape, cultural background and the psycho-emotional aspects of the people concerned. The planners and the implementing agencies should be aware of development. We must not forget that human and the available material resources are to be weighed correctly to bring about self-reliance and deterministic aptitude among people and all these combinedly must be transformed into a source of high creative activity. However, our study is not a fact-finding one. It is an attempt at identifying the inadequacies of design in the development of strategy, so that the activities can be streamlined. One should also realise the nature of harm done to the target groups who actually need immediate solution to overcome the stress and strain surging up every moment.

III

While considering about the development of these groups, specially the bigger ones, like the Lodhas and the Kharias, it may be said that the present CPI(M) dominated Government or the democratic bosses of the Panchayats have been consistently unmind ful to what happened to these people during all these years of democratic rule through the so-called welfare programmes (Rehabilitation Colony, Ashram Hostel or others). The nature or experience obtained from these and preparing a recipient vis-a-vis responsive mentality building in them is very important. The physical and socio-psychological condition of the people have completely been overlooked by the present District Tribal Advsory Committees while planning the welfare programmes. This sort of willful negligence or slipshod manner of dealing pushed the people again into misunderstanding. It appears that chauvinistic party-cadre areas are given the responsibility resulting in no development. The strong party bias towards development continues at the cost of the Central Government (public) money. Even the Ashram Hostels sanctioned earlier were not properly run, and today the school buildings, Ashram Hostels, constructed under earlier government are allowed to turn into shambles, *grain-golas* or grain-banks (Daharpur, Narayangarh Block) are dismantled and the material is sold in presence of Panchayat. This type of approach by the Panchayat Samity or the Zilla Parishad is, to say the least, is extremely reprehensible, but there is no way out. The authorities often tend to forget the adage : if the hut is not happy the palace is not safe. The bureaucratic apathy retards the pace of development and alienates people for whom the Central Government have liberally opened up their purse-strings.

It is seen that the Panchayat members having no experience, are empowered to sanction grants as and when they think it necessary. Money seems to have been spent for the sake of spending only, not to create any permanent good or get actual benefit. We suggest that the entire frame of the present day development programmes be changed, as it lacks in 'region specific development', or to create 'islands of development' and in effect gives a chance to the so-called overlords to misuse money and spoil the entire situation. If the beneficiary base is broadened, the back of the local political power-brokers in the Panchayat or the District Committees shall be effectively broken. These people are completely unaware that the government is running a Cultural Research Institute where some expert opinion can be had for the development. There are also experts in the University level, who are never consulted. This sort of lethargy or seeming ignorance is not expected of a democratic set up. The people remain at the stage where they were. Money and time are wasted. Such attitudes have created lots of disbelief and distrust among the people. They look at things with their unseeing eyes. Men having some sense of reality will certainly react to the situation in which tons of money go down the drain without any tangible result. The Government is maintaining a Hostel (Ashram) for tribal children. For the year 1990-91, hostel grant released after a long time. The resident students are allowed to go home. They will return only when money is available. Consequently nothing worth mentioning is expected in respect of education. These have created an absolutely demoralising ambience in which the group concerned are to suffer and some fortunate ones stand to gain.

Over this, there were continuously simmering discontent and unrest among many of the tribals, specially among the Lodhas, which led to a series of mass killing. All these are symptomatic and are the result of failures, spoiling of Central Government money, creation of more distrust and inability work for development.

IV

However, it is to be noted that for the small group, like the Totos or the Birhors, greater attention by the Government or the Panchayat is possible. But for the Lodhas and the Kharia or Kheria, it should be a treatment of different kind. The Lodha is suspected to a habitual criminals. Thus different tribes require different and distinct measures for development. It so happened that at one time a few lakhs of rupees was sanctioned by the Central Government for setting up an appropriate educational institution to train the Lodha children to overcome their age-old inhibitions. These children have had some psycho-emotional problems and, as such, a new environment setting was needed. But it is a matter of great regret that the money thus sanctioned was distributed to some other High Schools for establishing Hostels mentioned earlier (Table 6:5). The Narayangarh High School which never merited the grant received it on considerations best known to the authorities. Many more examples can be cited. Our simple and modest suggestions are : only to get the past lapses rectified to bring about the desired changes. We find considerable decentralisation of agencies in giving financial aids. The sanctioning and disbursing officers are to be made answerable and accountable to somebody above them and they must be made responsible for anything going wrong in the programme. The Panchayat functionaries have some set pattern of thinking about the welfare programmes. They are not in a position to bring the desired changes in the economic life of the people, to rationally utilise the available resources and to help people to cope with the new situation. New technology and education can bring changes motivating people to stop unwanted growth of population. Only such programmes with thrust on modern technology should be formulated. The Panchayat officers having no knowledge of meeting the grass-root needs plan and implement development programmes. The inevitable happens - failure and colossal waste. Nobody is there to question, nobody is accountable. Time flees away, money is squandered for nothing or for some temporary gain, and some crooks play a vital role to rob the less sophisticated for whom it is meant. The hopes of the people looking for security and satisfaction are dashed to be ground, in spite of the fact that the Government are pouring money to create new hopes, and aspirations to raise the self-confidence of the tribal people. The perpetrators are creating hydra-headed problems. The people remain ever discontented and disbelieving.

V

The welfare plan is originally prepared at the Panchayat level, through the Block Welfare Committee of the Panchayat Samity, and then the same is processed and finalised at the District Planning Cell and the State Planning Board, respectively. In all cases, the Panchayat Samity is the impementing authority.

The District Advisory Committee, i.e., the District Welfare Committee for the ST/SC and the Project Officer, I.T.D.P. aid and advise at the formulation level, but they are overshadowed by the elected office bearers. Very recently another Committee has been constituted for the development of the Primitive Tribal Groups with the General Manager of the District Industries Centre, the District Officer of the Khadi and Village Industries Board, as an apex body, who necessarily provide expert opinion and expertise to them. Of course, the decision of the Committee for the development of the P.T.G., is generally given clearance by the D.W.C. for SC/ST.

The beneficiaries are given the wherewithal as per plan, in cash or kind, by the functionaries of the Panchayat Samity. Funds are made available from the Centre through State and Zilla Parishad to be placed at the disposal of the Panchayat Samity for implementing various programmes.

The Panchayat Samity is the main implementing Agency which does work through the Gram Pradhan or by themselves, if they choose. Very recently, LAMPS are being encouraged and are involved in this job; and they are supposed to coordinate. There has been no occasion forever, when consultation with any expert body or individual was made. Hence, it appears that only grass-root level 'leaders' are virtually in charge of planning, disbursement of money and implementation of the work. As a result, the welfare activities generally fall through. Therefore, an evaluation and rethinking are very much necessary, to reorient the productive forces, the social relations and values.

Of course, development work is a symbol of hope and modernisation which throws the quality of life can be protected. However, while rethinking the welfare action programme, we shall have to emphasise to build a strong economic base by which the level of aspiration will be fixed at a high niche, overcoming all areas of maladjustments. Actually, hopes are dupes which do not soar higher and higher, and the people are multiplied without a corresponding increase in the new set up in the developmental strategy, sometimes bringing socio-political wirepulling with ulterior motive by the infighting groups. All these need to be understood for the overall development of the people. It is to be appreciated that the spirit of development thinking has changed, both in form and substance, which must be realised by the administrators.

VI

As it has been said earlier, that the development of the Primitive Tribal Groups require special considerations these are not all the time in tune with the general tribal welfare or the development procedures. Again, the Primitive Tribal Groups, a generic term which applies to 74 groups of people, some of whom live in different States. The actual number will be slightly less *i.e.*60 (Appendix-I) if we underscore the double counting. For example, the Lodhas in West Bengal, as well as in Orissa, are categorised at P.T.G., but not so in Bihar where they are less in number (about 800) and there they are designated as O.B.C. Nevertheless, these are administrative manoeuvrings. We need not bother about it. But it has been reiterated that there are some differences among the tribal groups. All these groups have different socio-economic and psycho-emotional problems and capabilities to respond at different degrees. The Totos living on the hill slopes are compartmentalised and sandwitched in between different ethnic groups and economic pressures, whereas the Birhors, living in the adjoining areas of Bihar, are a gathering-hunting tribe. The latter sustain on forest produce and typical case of culture of poverty. The Lodha, once a gathering hunting group, reluctant to do agriculture and is given to criminal activities. Though they still do some kind of collecting and gathering for a living, thieving as their regular habit of quite a few them. So their problem is different. The repeated mass killings of the Lodhas and burning of their huts by their neighbour make the Lodhas shaky, nervous and revengeful. So, to tackle tribals we shall have to consider three important factors :

1. the problems of the people who are problematic themselves;

2. the problem-creating neighbours consisting of the receivers of the stolen properties and those who employ them to create trouble for others; and lastly;

3. the problem administration which, without analysing the situation, believe in the statement of the Lodha.

To do substantially some good to the Lodhas, one has to understand these three aspects and fight the problem creating Lodha, his neighbours who use him and the administration which is often subjective.

The Kharia or Kheria have been considered along with the Lodhas, but actually they are two distinct groups.

Though they also live in the borders of the rugged terrain of Bengal, Bihar and Orissa; the Kharias are not stigmatized as criminal or de-notified tribe. They live on clandestine cutting trees and are not attracted to a stable and painstaking agricultural pursuit. Sections of this group living in other States do not pose the same problem. Reluctance to agriculture, and lure of the gathering--hunting habits is the problem regarding them. Only a section of the Hill Kharias of Bihar is categorised at P.T.G. all categories of the Kharias in Orissa are labelled as P.T.G. In West Bengal, they have been omitted **(Report of the Working Group on the Development and Welfare of the Scheduled Tribes During the Eighth Five Year Plan : 1990-1995 : Nov. 1989 : New Delhi).** Under such circumstances, the consideration and the development of the Kharias are to be taken up differently. However, the Report requests the authorities concerned to consider the group, as a whole (even if they are distributed in different States) and, as such they should be treated as P.T.G. in West Bengal to have all facilities for their betterment.

VII

Considering the nature of welfare or development programmes, with reference to West Bengal, we know that a good number of projects have proved to be failures. The economic projects (relating to all the categories) have not been able to make such dent on these groups of people. The planning has been faulty. These are exenditure reports, but not of the results. The Government records show that - Rs. 1,93,835 (vide 129 [IB] ITDP [JNR] dated 13.3.1984) was paid 'Printex Works' at Jhargram. The factory never received the money (Appendix-IV). There are many similar examples. The State Government or the Zilla Parishad, the Supreme Authority, for some mysterious reason and is satisfied in spite of no results and blisfully ignorant of the wastage of Government money in the name of welfare work. There are umpteen examples where the middle men or the contractors, in collusion with the authority managed to siphon funds through false vouchers indicating purchase of goats, etc. for beneficiaries in tribal development programmes. To bring any change in the economic condition of the people, a closer supervision and constant check are necessary.

Development should be area specific and tribe specific within area. Instead of spending laterally it is suggested that it should be aimed at to develop 'micro-growth centres' which ultimately create the spread effect in an around. Model growth centres, which having crop *cafeteria*, small scale industries, model schools and hostels, germ-free water, health, hygiene and first-aid arrangements etc. may have to be set up. It may be mentioned here that the Samaj Sevak Sangh activities centre at *Bidisa* (Appendix-V : NCERT Report), may be taken as a rough model. At this centre agricultural activities including kitchen gardening have strongly influenced the local people. With the co-operation of the Block Development Officer, and the Forest Department office, the social forestry scheme yielded good results in utilising the local resources and harnessing the local manpower throughout the year. The school dropouts can be yoked to different vocations.

The report emphatically suggests verification and to create intense development pockets instead of diluting the efforts over a large area to net the grant receiving creatures for the vote bank. It is suggested that plan be designed after proper assessment of the needs of the people and as far as possible, with experts advice drawn from the Universities, Research Institutes. The spending spree, through some middle-men in the name of development should be scrupulously eschewed.

There are Ashram Hostels, some of which are managed by the Panchayat, some by the school authorities and some are under the control of the voluntary organisations. The schools and the hostels run by the voluntary organisations are better managed. The hostels are maintained throughout the year. The Ashram Hostels for the P.T.G. students should have Balwadis or Creches organised and supported by the Central Government. The little pre-school children then can be socialisted to develop a school attending mentality. Some vocational training programme for dropouts should be run in the school complex to inculcate a sense of self-reliance among the school going youth. The Ashrams should have vegetable and flower gardens to combine beauty and utility. Again, it is suggested that all the hostels meant for the Primitive Tribal Groups must be controlled by the respective P.O.s (ITDP) at different places. In addition, a Refresher Course for the Primary Teachers attached to the schools and the Ashram Superintendents be organised from time to time to update their professional skill.

The apart, the scale of pay of the Superintendents, cooks, helpers, etc. should be standardised in comparison with the other States. Andhra Pradesh, Orissa the pay scale of the Ashram Superintendent is equal to that of a Primary School teacher and the pay of the cook is equal to that of fourth class staff. This aspect should be looked into.

The bright boys and girls of the P.T.G's should be transferred to good and reputed residential educational institutions, like the Ramakrishna Mission Schools or other such schools of the locality for better results and training to enable the bright children to show their mental and grit. It is also suggested that the Government (where State Government Funds or P.T.G Fund's) should take special care to repair all existing Hostels, Primary School buildings and provide such other items as furniture, equipment and bedding, etc. Electrification has to be extended to all Ashram Hostels. It is also suggested that there should be provision of excursion to the places of interest, as these will enlarge and widen their outlook and world-view.

Mobile Dispensary Units should visit all Ashram Hostels and Balwadis at regular intervals. Through them, a systematic concept of good health should be disseminated. All preventive medical care should be extended to the P.T.G's.

The Government should survey the nature of indebtedness and repayment to save the tribals from the clutches of the usurers and money lenders. Besides, there should be occasions when the tribal elders should be acquainted with the measures taken by the Government for their welfare.

Some Lodha employees with vested interest attached to ITDP, Jhargram, should be reverted to their original position and some other more enterprising person from a higher rank be placed there. The Lodha Social Workers who are attached to the office of the Block may be placed at the disposal of the Primary Schools in Tribal (Lodha) areas (as the pay-scale is the same) who will be able to watch the programmes in action.

All old colonies should be re-studied to see the possibility of developing them as micro-growth centres. Where the Family Benefit Scheme is being operated, a card system should be insisted upon. A copy of the card will remain with the owner, another with the Block level office and the third with the ITDP office. This will facilitate the process of considering their cases in respect of item-wise grants.

Lastly, we request the authorities concerned to develop a centre "Monitoring and Promoting Excellence". Crores of rupees is being spent, but there is no arrangement for monitoring all these projects. If the fruit-bearing trees/ plants scheme is unsccessful, why not an alternative scheme is offered to the group concerned ? In the same way, if goatery or milch-cow scheme fails, then an immediate switch over is to be made to an alternative on the basis of which projects will continue and will yield quick benefits to the group concerned. Besides, the members of the Monitoring Cell should be associated with the planning process. The members may be retired Government Officers from the Cultural Research Institute and University Departments of Anthropology, Geography, Economics having knowledge of tribal cultures.

The Director, Scheduled Castes and Scheduled Tribes Commission, Government of India, has no clear instructions of his supervisory duties. When the entire money is being spent by the Central Government it should also watch the performance. The Monitoring Centre may be attached to the Cultural Research Institute and be located at a suitable location.

Finally, the Lodhas and the Kharias of three States be covered by the same Monitoring Cell and its members be associated with the planning body.

The evaluation team had the advantage of meeting many officers who are at the helm of affairs who often answered our questions with evasive smiles, but could not answer satisfactorily about their performances. Welfare and development, till date, definitely failed to accrue the desired result. Now, time has come to rethink about it and to search for new alternatives to save time and money. The tribals should no longer be kept in an ocean of hopes and promises but, in reality like Tentalus, ever thirsty staying in water. This should go. A spirit of accommodation and involvement of many persons is needed for the cause of the down trodden suffering masses to develop a more integrated social order in the tune of *weltanschauung* of the intellectuals.

BIBLIOGRAPHY

BIBLIOGRAPHY

Balagopal, G. 1982. A Comprehensive Five Year Plant for the Development of the Toto Tribes.

Bhowmick, P.K. 1963. *The Lodhas of West Bengal,* Calcutta.

Bhowmick, P.K. 1975. Essential Primary Considerations for Rehabilitation Schemes. *Vanyajati*, Delhi.

Census of India, 1931, Government of India.

Census of India, 1961, Government of India.

Census of India, 1971, Government of India.

Census of India, 1981, Series 23. Special Tables for Scheduled Tribes. Part IX (iii) and Part X (iv).

Dalton, E.K. 1872. *Descriptive Ethnology of Bengal*. Government of Bengal Press, Calcutta.

Das, A.K. 1969. *The Totos*. Scheduled Caste and Tribal Welfare Department, Government of West Bengal, Calcutta.

Das, T.C. 1936. *The Wild Kharias of Dhalbhum*. Anthropological Paper No.3(1931) Calcutta, University of Calcutta-Reprinted from Paper No. 5. Journal of the Department of Letters, 30 (1985).

Dhali, D.N. 1987. *Toto* (in Bengali). C.R.I., Calcutta.

Dube, S.C. 1988. *Modernisation and Development, The Search for Alternative Paradigms,* Vistaar Publications, New Delhi.

Dubhasi, P.R. 1983. *Action Research for Development* in K.Mathur and Harsh Sethi, New Delhi.

Elwin, V.R. 1963. *A New Deal for Tribal India,* Ministry of Home Affairs, New Delhi.

Das, Roy and Chaudhury, 1982. *Planning the Scheduled Tribes and Scheduled Castes — A West Bengal Perspective.* CRI, Calcutta.

Roy, S.C. 1925. *The Birhors,* Ranchi.

Roy, S.C. and Roy, R.C. 1937. *The Kharias,* Ranchi.

Sanyal, C.C. 1955. *The Toto A Sub Himalayan Tribe.* Journal of the Asiatic Society of Bengal. Vol.21, No.2.

Sanyal, C.C. 1958. *Toto Revisited. Vanyajati.* Vol. 26, No. 4, Delhi.

Sanyal, C. 1973. *The Meches and The Toto—Two Sub Himalayan Tribes of West Bengal.* North Bengal University.

Sinha, D. 1984. *The Hill Kharias of Purulia, a Study on the Impact of Poverty on a Hunting and Gathering Tribe.* Anthropological Survey of India, Government of India, Calcutta.

Dhebar, U.N. 1961. *Report of the Scheduled Areas and Scheduled* Tribes Commission, Vol.1. New Delhi.

Tewari, D.N. 1984. *Primitive Tribes of Madhya Pradesh Strategy for Development.* Ministry of Home Affairs, Government of India. New Delhi.

Evaluation of Schemes Implemented for the Primitive Tribes in Maharashtra, 1984. Tribal Research and Training Institute, Maharashtra State, Pune.

Note on Primitive Tribal Groups of Andhra Pradesh and their Development 1987. Tribal Welfare Department, Government of Andhra Pradesh, Hyderabad.

Das, S. 1982. A Comparative Five-Year Plan for the Development of the Toto Tribes. The District Welfare Committee for the Scheduled Castes and Scheduled Tribes, Jalpaiguri, West Bengal.

Report of the Working Group on Development of Scheduled Tribes During Seventh Five-Year Plan, 1984. Ministry of Home Affairs, New Delhi.

Report of the Working Group on Development of Scheduled Tribes During Eighth Five-Year Plan, 1989. Ministry of Home Affairs, New Delhi.

Eighth Five-Year Plan of Midnapur District 1990-95. District Magistrate, Midnapur, Bengal.

Annual Action Plan 1990-91. Midnapur DRDA. Zilla Parishad Complex, Midnapur, West Bengal.

Evaluation Report on Integrated Tribal Development Projects. 1987. Planning Commission, Government of India, New Delhi.

APPENDIX

APPENDIX I

List of Primitive Tribal Groups of India

Sl. No.	*Name of the Primitive Tribal Group (PTG)*	*Distribution*
1.	Abuj Maria	- Madhya Pradesh
2.	Asura	- Bihar
3.	Baija	- Madhya Pradesh
4.	Bharia	- Madhya Pradesh
5.	Birhor	- Bihar, Madhya Pradesh, Orisa, West Bengal
6.	Birjia	- Bihar
7.	Bodo Gadaba	- Andhra Pradesh
8.	Bondo	- Orissa
9.	Bondo Paroja	- Andhra Pradesh
10.	Buxa	- Uttar Pradesh
11.	Chenchu	- Andhra Pradesh
12.	Cholanaikayan (a section of Ku Hunai ckans)	- Kerala

13.	Diyadi	- Orissa
14.	Dongaria Khond/ Dongria Khond	- Andhra Pradesh, Orissa
15.	Great Andamanese	- Andaman and Nicobar Islands
16.	Gutob Godaba	- Andhra Pradesh
17.	Hill Kharia/ Kheria	- Bihar (Hill Kharia), West Bengal, Orissa
18.	Hill Korba	- Madhya Pradesh
19.	Irula	- Tamil Nadu
20.	Jarawa	- Andaman and Nicobar Islands
21.	Jenu Kuraba	- Karnataka
22.	Juang	- Orissa
23.	Kadar	- Kerala
24.	Kamar	- Madhya Pradesh
25.	Kathods /Katkaria	- Gujarat, Maharashtra
	(Kathodia)	- Andhra Pradesh
26.	Khond Paroja	- Andhra Pradesh,
27.	Kolam	Maharashtra
28.	Kolgha	- Gujarat
29.	Konda Reddi	- Andhra Pradesh
30.	Koraga	- Karnataka, Kerala
31.	Korwas	- Bihar
32.	Kota	- Tamil Nadu
33.	Kotwalia	- Gujarat
34.	Kurumbas/Kurbmba	- Kerala, Tamil Nadu
35.	Kutia Kond/ Katia Khond	- Andhra Pradesh, Orissa
36.	Kuttunayakan/ Kattu Naikan	- Kerala, Tamil Nadu
37.	Langia Saora	- Orissa
38.	Lodha	- Orissa, West Bengal

39.	Mal Paharia	- Bihar
40.	Mantadia	- Orissa
41.	Maria Gond	- Maharashtra
42.	Marram Naga	- Manipur
43.	Onge	- Andaman & Nicobar Islands
44.	Padhar	- Gujarat
45.	Paharia	- Bihar
46.	Paniyan	- Tamil Nadu
47.	Pauri Bhuyan	- Orissa
48.	Porengi Paroja	- Uttar Pradesh
49.	Raji	- Andhra Pradesh
50.	Riang	- Tripura
51.	Saharia/Seharia	- Madhya Pradesh, Rajasthan
52.	Sauria Paharia	- Bihar
53.	Savar	- Bihar
54.	Sentenelese	- Andaman and Nicobar Islands
55.	Shompen	- Andaman and Nicobar Islands
56.	Siddi	- Gujarat
57.	Sour	- Orissa
58.	Thoti	- Andhra Pradesh
59.	Toda	- Tamil Nadu
60.	Toto	- West Bengal

APPENDIX II

(Out of Government Report)
Existing Assets Created (During 6th Plan)
ITDP Area

1. Agriculture Irrigation :	a)	Pump Sets	586 nos,
	b)	Dug Wells (R.C.C.)	61"
	c)	Shallow Tube Well.	511"
	d)	Re-excavation & Excavation of Tank	79 "
	e)	Soil Conservation	3000 Acres,
	f)	Diesel Hand Pump	31 Nos.
	g)	Construction of Bundhs	18 "
	h)	Gully plugging	200 "
	i)	Agri. implements	23,088 "
	j)	Constitution of Cause way over the river Tarafeni	1 "
	k)	Constn. of Bridge	3 "
	l)	Plough Cattle & Bullock Cart	810 "
2. Fishery:	a)	Air-breathing fish culture	310 tanks

3. Animal Husbandry :	a)	Distribution of cattle	300 nos.
	b)	Goatery	1100 "
	c)	Poultry Farm	1 "
4. Rural Water Supply :	a)	R.C.C. Wells	172 "
	b)	Tube Wells	127 "
5. Horticulture:	a)	Plantation of fruit-bearing trees	890 "
6. Housing :	a)	Repairing of houses	57 "
7. Tassar : Plantation	a)	Tassar Plantation	7.5 Hect.
Infra-structure Development	a)	Dev. of village roads	4 km.
	a)	Bakery centre	3 Nos.
	b)	Weaving centre	1 "
	c)	Knitting centre	1 "

APPENDIX III

Assets Created (since 1981 Upto 1989) For Development of Lodha Communities (Government Report)

S. No	*Name of Scheme*	*No.*	*No. of families benefited*
1.	Land Reforms [Reclamation]	2305.75 Acres.	5755
2.	Irrigation wells	332 Nos.	137
3.	Dug wells	127 "	127
4.	Tube wells	69 "	345
5.	(a) Drinking wells	68 "	1700
	(b) Tube-wells for drinking water	3 "	75
6.	Supply of bullocks	1614 "	1248
7.	Supply of goat.	7807 "	1874
8.	Supply of sheep	437 "	210
9.	Excavation of Tanks	5 Nos.	2

10.	Provision of shops	4 "	4
11.	Supply of seed, minikits & Agril. lmpl.	324 "	1324
12.	Community Centres	3 "	136
13.	Supply of fishing nets	10 "	72
14.	Supply of Sprayers/ Dusters	52 "	1560
15.	Cultivation of Babui	260 "	260
16.	Supply of Pump sets for irrign.	31 "	415
17.	Constn. of bundhs	7 "	140
18.	Poultry Farms	1 "	30
19.	Repair of Hostel buildings	3 "	60
20.	Tailoring Units	1 "	1
21.	Hostels for girls	3 "	20
22.	Printex	1 "	90
23.	Re-excavation of tanks	174 "	174
24.	Homeopathy Centres	6 "	750
25.	Supply of cows	845 "	645
26.	Pisciculture	174 " Pond	174
27.	Handloom	1 "	20
28.	Grant to Artisan	40 "	40
29.	Tassar cultivation	80 "	80
30.	Cots & beds	5 " Ashram Hostels	110
31.	Trolley & Rickshaw	90 " Families	90
32.	Mat Industry	105 " "	105
33.	Cultivation of Mat stick	105 " "	105

34.	Supply of grafts for fruit plants	1750 " "	1750
35.	Sup. of coconut and banana plants	1000 " "	1000

Quite a good no. of assets could be created but even then the standard of living of the tribal communities could not be improved over the years upto any standard level. Field enquiries and personal interviews with a sizable number of tribal people revealed that only a small number of the tribal families has been able to raise their income beyond the poverty line and to maintain the attained level of income. The factors, as identified, leading to such a sorry state of affairs are : lack of education, unresponsiveness of tribal people for change, preference for leisure and an attitude for reconciling with minimum needs, addiction to liquor, lack of co-ordination and monitoring at different levels.

The objectives and targets of I.T.D.P. Plans will be to implement schemes envisaged in the plans elfectively for attainment of objectives of I.T.D.P. in removing the imbalance in the economic development of the tribal people in order to ensure a better standard of living for them.

APPENDIX IV

Report : National Council for Educational Research and Training : Delhi

Bidisa - An Experiment in Tribal Development

Members of the Study Team

1. Prof. C.K. Basu — Convenor
2. Prof. H.B. Majumdar — Expert
3. Prof. R.K. Bhowmick — Innovator
4. Dr. B. Prakash — Social Worker, Attara
5. Miss P. Dasgupta — Lecturer, NCERT
6. Dr. B.R. Goyal — Lecturer, NCERT

Dates of Visit

Bidisa is an institution devoted to uplift of Lodhas, an ex-criminal tribe of West Bengal. It aims at enculturation of these tribes in the mainstream of Indian society. It has been successful in achieving social transformation and within a short period, the nomadic, criminal 'food gatherers' have settled as `food growers' and have been socialized. The social workers of Bidisa, mostly constituting anthropologists, sociologists, psychologists and teachers, have shared the 'grim and gay' of the tribal life in their attempts to civilize the uncivilized develop a scientific outlook in them. This report aims at presenting a brief sketch of the various phases of the progress of this institute.

Bidisa is called an 'Ashram' by the local people. It is in District Midnapur and is situated at a distance of about 19 kms. at the roadside on the Orissa Trunk Road from Kharagpur in West Bengal. It is managed by the 'Samaj Sevak Sangha' a registered voluntary organisation. Late N.K. Bose would send his scholars to study the life and culture of the tribal people. One of his students, Dr. P.K. Bhowmick, presently the Head of the Department of Anthropology, Calcutta University, had gone to collect information about Lodhas of District Midnapur, West Bengal. He was manhandled by the criminals and he reflected that education does not merely lie in 'knowing about the underprivileged' rather it in 'doing something for the uplift of the underprivileged'. Thereafter, he decided to dedicate his services for causing social uplift, economic amelioration and educational progress in the tribal people of the area. Consequently, the institute was founded.

Objectives

Bidisa is a Sanskrit word symbolic of 'Causing Culture'. It speaks of the task before the innovator to bring social transformation in an undeveloped tribe. In consonance with the aim, the following objectives were envisaged:

(i) to give an economic footing to the poverty stricken, landless, nomadic and criminal tribes;

(ii) to socialize them in order to bring them in mainstream of Indian society by inculcating in them the values of the middle class; and

(iii) to cause education in them.

Description of Activities

A two pronged approach was adopted for achieving the objectives viz. introduction of economic activities for the adults and opening of school for the children. In order to interest parents in the education of their children flexibility in the curriculum was created to relate education with productivity and work experience. Agricultural crafts were introduced. By and by programmes focussed on the tribal's problems-food, clothing and shelter were developed. The agricultural crafts were later on supplemented with horticulture, carpentary, weaving, spinning and tailoring. Later on, spinning was droped for its expensiveness.

The tribal people were superstitious to an extent that for mere cold and cough, they would sacrifice the pets for pleasing the spirits. The school took up programmes of cleanliness, sanitation and health. Modern medical preventives of diseases, and epidemics were introduced. The people were reluctant in the beginning but gradually developed faith in the newer medical practices.

The Educational Programmes

The primary school established in 1961 has grown into a residential high school now. In the initial stages there was social resistance to admission of pupils and the school had to create flexibility in the content, timings and methods of teaching. Parents were persuaded to send children. Free books, uniforms were supplied, provision of mid-day meals was made. Even hostel facilities were created. The school appeared to be a noval place for the children. Those who once roamed in wildness and who had never seen the corners and boundaries found it difficult to stay within the four walls of the classroom and the boundary walls of the school. Some of the queer experiences were such as the following:

(i) Children took the mosquito nets stealthily to the ponds and tried to fish;

(ii) They made bonfire of their uniforms for fun;

(iii) They escaped at night, roamed over miles in darkness and slipped back before it was dawn;

(iv) They sold the food to get intoxicants and tobacco; and

(v) They sorted the dormictory

The above experiences are quoted as examples to show that a human being takes time in adapting to facilities and therefore, the process of social transformation should be slow but gradual. If it was so in the case of young children, how much strenous and thrilling it would have been to the adult men and women to settled down in habitations is left to the reader's imagination but surely it was always a test to the patience of the innovator and his team of social workers.

The untamed children were gradually socialised by introducing an extensive programme of games and sports, climbing up the trees, swimming, arranging excursions and picnics. In other words, the transition from the outside world to the inside of the classroom was through outdoor activities. One of the features of the innovation was to create an effect of beauty in productivity leading to utility. This helped in the sustenance of children's interests.

Adult Education Programmes

By the year 1966 the Government of West Bengal extended financial assistance for the development of Bidisa.

A grant for the erection of hostel was released by the Tribal Welfare Department. Senior Basic School upto Class VIII had been opened in the Ashram in 1968. Two Balwadis are functioning to look after the growth of the children. The concrete work done by the school had attracted parents. They had shed off their timidity after seeing the police and govt. officials appreciating their children. It was time for the staff to take up further work in the habitations. Agriculture, carpentry, weaving were introduced. One pumpingset was installed. The young women folk were given a sewing machine and taught needle work and tailoring. A cooperative was established. The team of activities attracted other tribes viz. Santals and Mundas, to share education and cultivation facilities and today in the vicinity to Ashram, the three tribes meet. The entire social environment around the Ashram, speaks of the closeness of a family.

The task of social transformation is thorny too. Unless the purposeful activities are assimilated as attitudes and habits, they can lapse back into antisocial activities. The Lodhas, sometimes, sell the milching cattle for community feasts and they invite poverty. In March, 1968, there was a riot among Lodhas and the Santals and Mahatos. The financial difficulties very soon tend to overcome the achievements and there have been so many instances when the social workers had to postpone work for want of money. As a safeguard, more land was procured and brought into cultivation. Senior boys were trained in better methods of agriculture and assigned agricultural activities as a compulsory part of their education. The teachers and the students joined hands in diffusing the knowledge of better agricultural practices to the tribes. New variety of seeds and chemical fertilizers were introduced. A night school for women was established to accelerate the pace of progress, the Lodhas are almost self-sufficient.

The developments in the Ashram attracted the attention of scholars and it is now the field station of the Institute of Social Research and Applied Anthropology, Department of Anthropology, Calcutta University.

The management of the Samaj Sevak Sangha have not undertaken any evaluation of their work. According to them, there cannot be a terminal stage in social transformation. But the changing environment, replacement of wild bushes by sheaves of wheat and paddy, shedding of superstition and sluggishness, admission of more and more children to the school, increase in the number of cattle and above all the smiles on the faces of all people, young and old, are an index of their increasing success. They have to enculturate a tribe that had never known progress with the progress of mankind achieved after thousands of years of effort. They are on their way. Presently one of the Ashram boys has matriculated and got employment as a teacher. He is, perhaps, the first teacher in Lodha Community. The community and the Ashram are so proud of this boy whom they call as their own teacher.

Index